# PARENTING
## *beyond*
# PINK & BLUE

# PARENTING *beyond* PINK & BLUE

How to Raise Your Kids Free
of Gender Stereotypes

**CHRISTIA SPEARS BROWN, PHD**

Ten Speed Press
BERKELEY

**TO ALEX BROWN,** an extraordinary man, for helping me
become a developmental psychologist, a mom, and a better human

**TO KRIS KEARNS,** a remarkable husband and dad, for encouraging this
book, putting up with my antics, and showing up every day

**TO MAYA AND GRACE,** two completely unique daughters, for teaching
me how heartwarming and heart-wrenching parenting can be

Published in the United States by Ten Speed Press, an imprint of the Crown Publishing
Group, a division of Random House LLC, a Penguin Random House Company, New York.
www.crownpublishing.com
www.tenspeed.com

Ten Speed Press and the Ten Speed Press colophon are registered
trademarks of Random House LLC

Brown, Christia Spears.
 Parenting beyond pink and blue : how to raise your kids free of gender stereotypes /
Christia Spears Brown, PhD. -- First edition.
   pages cm
 ISBN 978-1-60774-502-0 (pbk)
 1. Parenting. 2. Stereotypes (Social psychology) 3. Sex role. 4. Sex differences
(Psychology) I. Title.
 HQ755.8.B763 2014
 649'.1--dc 3
                        2014001259

Trade Paperback ISBN: 978-1-60774-502-0
eBook ISBN: 978-1-60774-503-7

Printed in the United States of America

Design by Sarah Adelman

10 9 8 7 6 5 4 3 2 1

First Edition

# Contents

# Acknowledgments

I would like to extend thanks to several people who have helped this book come to fruition. Thanks to Professors Rebecca Bigler and Campbell Leaper, two mentors and colleagues who have deeply shaped my research and thinking about gender stereotypes and the importance of parenting. Thanks to my closest friend and colleague, Professor Rashmita Mistry, for providing moral support and encouragement through this process (and patience when I bogged down our other work). Thanks to Professor Ellen Usher for reading early drafts of the manuscript and offering extremely helpful feedback. Thanks to my colleagues at the University of Kentucky (particularly in my own Psychology Department, but also colleagues in Education and Sociology) who have listened to me talk about this topic for years, both formally and informally, and encouraged me throughout. Thanks to my editor Sara Golski at Ten Speed Press for being enthusiastic about the message behind this book and helping me write the message more clearly. Thanks to my literary agent, Linda Konner, for providing mounds of helpful advice and advocacy at every stage of this process, thoughtful feedback and edits, and general guidance for this newcomer.

Closer to home, I am very grateful to the graduate and undergraduate students in the Children's Social Identity and Inequality Research Lab, from 2003 to today. They have helped me talk about these topics in academic words and real words and helped me maintain my passion for the subject. Jordan Carr spent her evenings keeping track of all the studies I cited and turned jumbled notes into an organized reference section. A special thanks to Jennifer A. Jewell, a gender researcher herself, for running my research lab and supervising students while I dropped out of sight to write this book.

Last, enormous thanks to my husband, Kris Kearns, for listening to almost every word of this and telling me when it didn't make sense.

# Prologue

# On Being the
# Weird Daughter-in-Law

**I am the weird daughter-in-law.** I know it and have learned to embrace it. I first realized it when I overheard my sister-in-law whisper to my niece, "Let's put that away. Aunt Christy won't like it." She was right. It was one of those light-up mirrors that girls use when they pretend to put on makeup. This pink plastic mirror came with plastic makeup and hair care products—and a voice. My skin crawled when it said, "You sure look pretty with that makeup on" or "Wow, your hair looks great!"

I quickly told my niece, who loves this makeup mirror, that I think she looks pretty all the time and that she is smart, funny, and interesting, which is even more important. Although I have no memory of it, my sister-in-law swears I took the batteries out of the mirror so that it couldn't talk anymore. I am not saying I didn't do it, and that is kind of my M.O.—the subversive editing out of gender stereotypes.

I used to do this often, quietly undoing as many gender stereotypes as I could in my children's lives. After a while, I wasn't so quiet. In my house, there is an explicit ban on pants with words written on the butt (I am not sure why someone thought it was a good idea for people to stare at the butt of a seven-year-old). My family knows about my hatred of Barbie (although she still sometimes sneaks in during Christmas). I often pull my older daughter, Maya, aside and say, "Just because Grandma thinks boys are stronger than girls doesn't mean it is true."

When Maya got the latest Barbie doll for her birthday, I remembered the experiment that found that girls who were given a Barbie to play with had a more negative view of their body and weight than girls who were given a more realistic doll. When she got the latest Disney princess movie, I mentally replayed the documentary *Mickey Mouse Monopoly*. In it, a ten-year-old girl innocently states, in response to what she learned by watching *Beauty and the Beast*, that she should just be nice to her boyfriend, even when he is mean to her (statistics about teen dating violence flashed through my head). So several birthday presents get "lost" in the trashcan between the party and the house.

Part of my problem is that I don't want to be the weird mom or daughter-in-law, nor do I want my daughters to be "the weird kids." I don't want to put "No Barbies" on their birthday party invitations. I know some people will give Maya Barbies, but I also know that Maya will get other toys she'll enjoy too, and that she's never once missed or asked about a disappearing Barbie. All of this has me walking the fine line between stereotypes and social acceptance.

I also struggle because the biggest proponents of gender stereotypes, the biggest consumers of gender-typed toys, media, and clothes, are the caring, sweet women who love my children dearly. I have been blessed with parents and in-laws who are wonderful people. They are a challenge because they are kind people who mean no harm. One mother-in-law now just attaches the receipt with every gift in case I want to return it. So I try to edit out gender stereotypes without offending people. I can handle being thought of as weird, but I never want to be thought of as rude.

To back up a bit, I didn't start out this way. When I first got married, I didn't pay much attention to gender. I was young and childless and a recent college graduate. I was working with at-risk children in inner city schools and trying to figure out what I wanted to study in graduate school. And then my life changed on a Saturday afternoon at McDonald's.

I was in the drive-thru ordering a Happy Meal when the speaker blasted, "A boy or a girl?"

"Huh?" I said (I'd been expecting a question about ketchup or napkins).

She repeated her question, clearly irritated that I wasn't going along with the script. "Why does it matter?" I asked. "So we know what toy to put in it," she said. At that moment, I was struck by what a pointless question this was.

I drove home with my mental wheels turning: "How does knowing if it's a boy or girl tell you what toy a kid will like?" "Why can't you just ask 'Do you want the My Little Pony or Legos?'" "How often do we base our decisions on someone's gender?" And most importantly, "Does this affect who children turn out to be?"

So, for the price of a Happy Meal, I now had a career goal. I needed to answer those questions. I went to graduate school, earned a PhD in developmental psychology, and specialized in how our obsession with gender and the differences between boys and girls affects children and their development. My eyes were opened to the many ways our society focuses on gender, even when it is irrelevant. I learned about how children socialize themselves to fit in with their same-gender group. I studied and conducted research on the damage gender stereotypes exact on boys and girls.

When I became a mom, my studies took on a whole new level of importance—and complexity.

When my first child, Maya, was very young, it was easy to focus on my goal of having a stereotype-free home. Lots of time and energy went into editing out the gender stereotypes around us. I would substitute the word "kid" in books when the author wrote "boys" or "girls," I would tear out "Peter Peter Pumpkin Eater, had a wife and couldn't keep her" from the Mother Goose books, and I would only buy blue and green clothes to balance out all the pink clothes given to us.

My parenting style has relaxed a bit now, mainly because I also wanted to avoid making Maya the freaky social outcast who had never heard of Disney movies. My desire to raise a child without gender stereotypes was balanced by my desire to raise a child with friends and good social skills. Also, these struggles became more complex as Maya's very stereotypically girly friends started to have a powerful influence. I remember the painful day she marched home and proudly announced that her favorite color was no longer green but pink. This change was driven more by her desire to be like her best friend, Dakota, than anything else.

With my second daughter, Grace, my commitment to gender-blind parenting took on a different flavor, mainly because Grace was so different from Maya, and the unique characteristics I wanted to foster were different. I am reminded daily of how much variability there is between children, even when both are girls. Despite their similarities, they are different at their core. But I also suffer the same kind of fatigue everyone feels with a second child. I have less energy now to edit out every stereotype I find in a book or toy. I pick and choose my battles more often.

This book bridges what I know as a developmental psychologist with what I face trying to raise children in our society. It is a look at our cultural obsession with gender. I describe the science behind why we form stereotypes, how to know when those stereotypes are accurate and when they are misguided, and how those stereotypes affect boys and girls. I also describe the difficulties—and rewards—of parenting against the norm and why I think it is ultimately worth the fight.

The book is organized in three parts. Part I describes how we use gender constantly to sort, categorize, and label children and how that affects our thinking about people, including our own kids. Part II describes how that gender focus is, more often than not, inaccurate, and how most of our presumed gender differences are really more stereotype than science. Part III describes how our focus on gender differences can actually affect our own kids in the real world, how it can limit their strengths and abilities, and how you can realistically parent with a little less focus on gender and a little more focus on your individual children (without making your mother-in-law think you are a total nut job). With this approach, children can be more secure, happier, more well-rounded, and better able to reach their full potential (and it can be a lot more fun for parents).

My goal in this book isn't to convert everyone to my exact way of parenting. My goal is to help parents know what science really tells us about gender differences; to think about the ways parents understand and explain their children's behavior; to spend a few extra seconds before making a decision about what activities to enroll their children in; to think twice about believing that any difference between their son and daughter is entirely due to gender; to not always say, "You know how boys are." Basically, I hope this book can help parents recognize and foster their children's unique strengths, even in a culture obsessed with fitting everyone into a pink or blue box.

PART I

# GENDER DIFFERENCES: CHANGING OUR FOCUS

## CHAPTER 1

# Noticing Gender

**The ordinary things that surround us** every day rarely catch our attention. It's why the old brainteaser, Which way does Lincoln face on the penny?, works (most people don't know). As humans, we don't walk around thinking about the air. We just breathe. Gender is the same way. It is ubiquitous and unnoticed, and much of the time, it goes unquestioned.

Let's start with a snapshot of the ways in which we label, stereotype, categorize, and thereby create a gender-focused world for ourselves. See if these examples ring true in your experience, or perhaps even in your household. In later chapters, we'll get to the nitty-gritty of why and how we stereotype and label. For now, let's just take a good look at what we're up against.

It begins with the first signs of the baby bump. One of the very first questions a parent-to-be is asked is "What are you having?" My smartass response, "A baby," was always met with blank stares and a polite smile. Parents often wait to decorate the baby's room or buy toys until they know the baby's gender. A *How I Met Your Mother* TV episode played off this need to know by joking that Marshall and Lily had to find out the gender of their baby or else the baby would be forced to wear the only gender-neutral outfit available: a burlap sack.

If you must know your child's gender in advance, you can buy a baby gender predictor kit from Intelligender.com. Or, for free, you can examine the ever-popular and Internet-friendly Chinese Gender Chart based on the mother's age and the month you conceived. According to this, I should have two boys, instead of the two girls I actually had. There is also the oft-mentioned, "You are carrying so low, it must be a boy." I was told this many times (again, those two daughters I had would disagree). I always responded, "I am 5'3". Everything I carry is low."

Folklore is full of ways to guess a baby's gender. You are likely to have a boy if your baby's heartbeat is lower than 140 beats per minute; you carry in the front; you don't have morning sickness; you crave salty foods; your right breast is larger than your left one; you tie your wedding ring to some thread, hang it over your stomach, and it moves in circles; or my personal favorite, you were the more aggressive partner during the "conception phase" of pregnancy. You are likely to have a girl, according to my hairdresser at least, if your hair looks terrible and your face breaks out. In her words, "Girls steal your beauty." Maybe she was trying to comfort me while I complained about my frizzy hair and recent breakout of zits. Girls are also predicted, according to folklore, if you carry high, have a larger left breast, crave sweet things, lie on your right side while you sleep (which must be hard with that large left breast), or have dull yellow urine. Apparently, ever since babies first gestated, people have been trying to predict gender.

If you have a preference for a gender, there are millions of tricks for changing the odds of having a boy or a girl—for example, stand on your head, have sex with your pelvis raised, do forty-one jumping jacks, turn around three times fast, and yell out the name of your childhood pet.

Why all this fascination with knowing the gender of your baby? There seems to be more to it than what color to paint the nursery. Rather, we assume that knowing the gender will tell us what our future holds for parenting: "Will I attend Little League games?" "Will I have to go to the mall?" "Will I spend my time playing with Nerf guns or Easy-Bake Ovens?"

My husband's first response to finding out we were having a girl was "I really hate playing with a doll house. It's so boring." He automatically assumed that a girl equals a life of Barbie Dream Houses. I reminded him that I think that stuff is boring too and suggested he could teach our daughter to do the things he finds interesting.

But whenever I feel crabby about the overuse of gender as a defining characteristic, I realize that, as an American, I shouldn't complain too much. It could be worse. At least in the United States, birth rates don't differ much based on a baby's gender. In China, there are 119 boys born for every 100 girls because of the use of gender-specific abortions. Some people care so much about the gender of their baby, they abort the ones they don't want (the gender imbalance signifies which is the preferred baby). So I do keep my husband's brief grimace in perspective.

## Great Expectations

If you are pregnant, think about what your expectations are for your baby. Do they differ based on whether your child is a boy or girl? If so, ask yourself why. You may expect life to be different if you are having a boy versus having a girl. Sure, it can differ. You could spend a life at ballet classes, American Girl stores, and shopping for princess costumes if you have a girl, and basketball games, the Lego store, and shopping for Nerf guns if you have a boy. But that is up to you. You and your coparent can bring your own interests into the life of your child, no matter what the gender. I personally hate playing with dolls. So I don't do that with my kids. We do other fun stuff, like cooking or nature hunts. My husband, who is never happier than when he's at a boat show, has instilled in Maya an interest in cars and boats.

# A GENDER-COLORED WORLD

Our obsession with gender only increases after the little one is born. In the hospital, babies are given a pink or blue blanket. They come home in a pink or blue car seat that gets clicked into a pink or blue stroller, and they sleep on pink or blue sheets in their pink or blue room. Boys cuddle up to stuffed cars and trains, and girls have their "My First Baby" waiting in their nurseries.

We do a lot to ensure that other people see the gender of our children. Notice all of the baby boys sporting a "Daddy's Little Man" onesie. Also popular, "Daddy's Lil' Slugger," "Daddy's Big Helper," or "Daddy's Future All-Star." For the parent who wants to appear outside the norm, but clearly isn't, you can buy a boy's onesie on eBay that reads, "I Love Tattooed Chicks." Girls get plenty of Daddy love via onesies, too. They can be branded as "Daddy's Precious Angel" or "Daddy's Princess." Or just ask the poor bald babies whose mothers insist on taping a bow to their shiny bald heads so everyone knows they are girls.

Because of my aversion to taped-on bows, and my tendency to have very bald children, people frequently called Grace a boy. Although her stroller was light blue, her clothes were often pink thanks to her grandmothers' frequent shopping sprees. But the bald head seemed to throw people off. Well-meaning strangers would frequently say, "He is so cute. What's his name?" I would smile and respond, "Thanks. Her name is Grace." I could see the look of horror come over their faces as they realized their terrible error. Their thought bubble would read, "OH MY GOD, I called their girl a boy. Fix it, fix it." They would then profusely apologize and backpedal, saying, "Of course, she is a girl. She looks totally like a girl. . . ." It was as though they had accidentally called her stupid and ugly.

From the beginning, gender consciousness drives every purchase we make. Even the gender-neutral toys that both boys and girls enjoy, like bikes, come in two versions: one pastel version, usually pink or purple, and one bright version, usually blue or red. The popular Fisher Price

Little People school bus, with the plastic kids and bus driver, which was always logically school bus yellow, now comes in a pink version.

The same goes for Legos. In 2012, Legos started more aggressively marketing to girls. What does that mean? Of course, they now come in pink and purple and have templates to build kitchens, hair salons, and shopping malls. One Legos kit clearly marketed to girls is called "Belleville" and features a horse. Apparently Legos is a boys' toy, so in an attempt to attract girls, they made a version for girls. At some point, primary colors were co-opted by boys and pastel colors co-opted by girls.

It is hard for a parent to avoid being influenced by gender while shopping. Most stores, even online stores, are divided into a boys section and a girls section. To buy a toy that doesn't fit your child's "category," you literally have to cross the aisle. As a parent of girls, I have wandered the aisles of action figures and cars to find what I am looking for. I recall online shopping for a toy workbench for Maya as a toddler and having to click the "boys' toys" link. Even I felt weird about that; most parents of daughters wouldn't do that, I thought. From my experience, it is even less likely that parents of boys would click the "girls' toys" link to buy a doll, and very rarely would they ever shop the pink aisle at Target, no matter how committed they are to gender equality.

## BOYS ON THE RIGHT, GIRLS ON THE LEFT

Once children enter preschool and then elementary school, the emphasis on gender increases. Children enter the classroom: Their birthdays are listed on the bulletin board with a pink face or blue face. They line up boy-girl-boy-girl. Several years ago, I was in a math class of fourth graders and the teacher had them go to the board boy-girl-boy-girl to solve math problems (when you read chapter 10, you will understand my frustration with this particular use of gender). In most schools, gender gets used regularly in physical education classes. And it isn't simply about boys versus girls in a game of dodgeball. Boys are often asked to do more sit-ups and push-ups than girls, even though most elementary school girls are bigger and stronger than their male peers (because they develop at a slightly faster rate).

## Reflection

Because our use of gender is so ubiquitous, we rarely really notice it. I know I never thought twice about my high school graduation where I wore a white cap and gown and my male classmates wore red ones. At Maya's chorus performance, the girls wore red shirts and the boys wore black shirts. Think back on your own life, and look around your kids' lives. How often were you sorted, categorized, or color-coded based on gender? Interestingly, because this trend is growing, it probably happens more in your kids' lives than it did in yours.

Kids often segregate themselves, and adults are happy to sanction the division. My husband had lunch with Maya recently at school and commented that all the girls sat at one lunch table and all the boys sat at another. When he asked Maya why this was, she said that it was their assigned seating. She never questioned the logic of this segregation.

The first time this adult-sanctioned segregation really hit home for me was when Maya was in the first grade and a classmate's mom asked me if we were going to a certain birthday party. We had never received an invitation, but I knew Maya and the birthday boy were friends. We had gone the year before, and the same kids seemed to go to the same birthday parties. I assumed Maya might have lost the invitation on the way home from school. When I casually asked around, I realized what had happened. It was a boys-only party. At first, I didn't think much of it. Maybe the parents could only afford to host a few kids and this was a way to cut down on the guest list. The real reason was more revealing. The birthday boy was having a pirate-themed party, and his mom assumed that girls would not be interested.

A friend recently told me about her niece's "gender-themed" birthday party. It was a girls-only invitation, and the party was held at an accessories store. The ten-year-old birthday girl's mom distributed $10 gift cards to the partygoers, who got to shop for two hours for bracelets, rings, and hair bows. Granted, I don't know any boys who would like to do this for two hours. But I also know plenty of girls who would be bored with this kind of party after five minutes.

Just like with the Happy Meal toy, we assume interests—like pirates versus bracelets—based solely on whether there is a G or B written after each child's name. And on the strength of gender alone, adults segregate kids into activities they think the child would like (or, perhaps even more often, what they think their child would not like).

## NOT JUST KIDS' PLAY

Our obsession with gender doesn't end in childhood, of course. Adults frequently use gender to sort out the world. Your gender is part of your label if, say, you win best actor or actress at the Academy Awards, or worst actor or actress the Razzies. Your gender is part of your label when you use a public bathroom. Magazine racks are divided into and labeled "men's interests" and "women's interests." Apparently, according to this marketing approach, men like cars and women like pie.

It is common to embed gender in our language, ladies and gentlemen. Even though it is more difficult to say, I always refer to my husband as a "firefighter" instead of a "fireman." Children's school days often start with "Good morning, boys and girls." We continue to emphasize gender with every "What a smart girl" and "What a big boy you are" comment we make. We have even figured out how to use gender as an insult. Not even a girl wants to "throw like a girl." Particularly damaging is the insult that someone "cries like a little girl." This insult actually hurts boys more than girls, implying that their natural reaction to something sad or hurtful is wrong.

We emphasize, label, sort, decide, and judge based on gender, regardless of its relevancy to the situation. There are counterarguments, of

course. Here are the ones I hear most often when I talk about our obses-
sive labeling and sorting by gender: "We are different." "It isn't bad to
treat groups differently that clearly look different." "It is the way it has
always been." That last one is my favorite argument; the "way it has
always been" is a close cousin of "Well, that's just the way it is."

The clearest rebuttal I have—beyond the decades of research showing that labeling matters (more on that in chapter 2)—is to acknowl-
edge that we do look different and, in many ways, are different. But we
aren't different in as many ways as we imagine (see chapters 4 and 5).
More to the point, just because we have always labeled and sorted by
gender doesn't mean we always have to.

We have always been fans of sorting people into categories (we'll
come back to this tendency in chapter 2). We have a history of labeling
and sorting on the basis of another physical difference—race. African-
Americans alive prior to the Civil Rights movement remember that all
too well. Jim Crow laws are illegal now, yet we used to think that was
the way it always was and always would be. No one would dream of
starting class with "Good morning, White and Black kids. Let's line up
White, Black, Latino, White, Black, Latino." Maya Angelou (my Maya's
namesake) said, "When you know better, you do better." When it comes
to using race categories, we now know better (at least, most of us do).
With gender, we are still learning.

## PRINCIPLES, IN MODERATION

How far do we take gender-blind parenting? A very few parents go
to the extreme. In 2011, several of my friends and students told me
about a news story from the *Toronto Star* regarding a Canadian child
named Storm. Storm's parents decided not to tell anyone what their
child's gender was. According to Storm's parents, "We've decided not
to share Storm's sex for now—a tribute to freedom and choice in place
of limitation, a stand up to what the world could become in Storm's
lifetime (a more progressive place?)." The parents weren't even telling

the grandparents the gender of their new baby. They wanted people to interact with their child free of expectations and stereotypes. They referred to their baby as Storm and never as he or she. Storm is tired, Storm is taking a nap, Storm is eating peas, Storm is probably sick of hearing Storm's name.

I can only imagine trying to pull that with my in-laws and parents. I am certain my baby would have been hijacked from her crib and de-diapered. But as Storm's mom puts it, "If you really want to get to know someone, you don't ask what's between their legs." (*Toronto Star*, May 21, 2011.)

When this story hit the news, lots of people asked me what I thought about it. I found the situation fascinating for many reasons. I think Storm's parents are completely right in their principles. The point of this book is that we shouldn't judge people by their gender. But I also wouldn't do this to my kids. I believe in principles, but I also want my children to have friends and not get pummeled at school, which is often the case for children who veer too far outside the norm. And that is another goal of this book: to de-emphasize gender in dealing with individual children but to recognize—and work with—the world we live in.

## THE FINAL FOUR: WHAT ARE THE KEY ISSUES?

- We constantly use gender to label, sort, categorize, and segregate people. Think about how many times an individual's gender comes up when we talk about him or her (see, it's difficult to even write one sentence without dealing with gender).

- We constantly color-code our children, segregate them by gender based on presumed interests, and use their gender to make decisions for them. This starts in the womb.

- We are really bothered if we believe a child is accidentally placed in the wrong category. Why does this matter? Is accidentally calling a boy a girl, or a girl a boy, an insult?

- Is this constant use of gender to label and sort people necessary? Would the world fall apart if girls weren't always in pink or boys in blue?

## "Using" Gender at Home

How do you "use" gender in your own parenting? We all do it sometimes, because it is so hard to avoid completely:

- Do you color-code your purchases so that, given two options, you buy the pink one for your daughter or the blue one for your son?

- Do you say things like "What a strong boy!" or "What a big girl!"?

- Do you include gender in your compliments (or criticisms) of your kids?

- Do you invite only girls or only boys to your young child's birthday party? (It's a very different issue with parties for kids who have reached puberty, especially if sleepovers are involved.)

- Do you say things within earshot of your kids, like "You know how boys are," or "Boys will be boys," or, as in my husband's case, "Life is crazy in a house full of women!"?

- Do you automatically only shop in the pink or blue aisle of the toy store, regardless of what you are looking for?

## CHAPTER 2

# Why Labels Matter

**If you didn't before, you are now** starting to recognize how often we label and sort people based on their gender. We do this to everyone, young and old, but we save our most intense sorting for young children. Infants and children in preschool are the ones most likely to be color-coded and talked about with some reference to their gender. Unfortunately, this is the worst possible age to focus on gender so intensely. This is the age when children are highly focused on adults so that they can learn about the world.

Most people assume that labeling and sorting by gender doesn't really matter, that it doesn't lead to big differences between boys and girls, as long as you treat children equally. That argument makes sense. We are always taught that it is how you treat a person that counts. This is a key tenet in every religious and moral code in the world, some version of "Treat others how you want to be treated" (and, of course, we all want to be treated with kindness and fairness).

That assumption—that labeling and sorting children based on gender doesn't really matter as long as everyone is treated fairly—would hold true if children only paid attention to the more overt, obvious messages we adults send. If children only listened to our purposeful messages, parenting would be easy. Most (but not all) parents and teachers take great effort in treating their children fairly, regardless of gender. Parents don't need to say to their daughters, "You probably won't enjoy math" or say to their sons, "Real boys don't play with dolls." Most parents wouldn't dream of saying these blatant stereotypes to their kids. But research has shown that when we label (and sort and color-code) by gender, children do notice. And it matters—children are learning whether you mean to be teaching them or not.

## IT'S ELEMENTARY

Children are detectives, Sherlock Holmeses clad in OshKosh B'gosh. They pick up on subtle cues from the world around them about what is important. They are observant and voracious consumers of all that adults do. This is how they learn about the world, after all.

Take an example not related to gender: language development. Children learn an entire language before starting school just by paying close attention to the words others use. To be more specific, by age two, children can say several hundred words. Their understanding of language happens even earlier. This happens regardless of which language the child speaks, and it happens earlier in childhood when parents speak to their child frequently and consistently.

What are the two tricks parents use to help their child learn a language (tricks they are probably not even aware they are using)? First, they talk to their babies in a special voice designed to capture the child's attention. This is sometimes called motherese. It is that high-pitched, simple, and slow speech that everyone seems to do instinctively when talking to babies.

Second, parents label everything. I caught myself doing that with Grace all the time when she was a baby. She picked up a spoon, and I would say, "That's your spoon." We would see a bus drive by, and I would say, "There goes the school bus." She pottied in her potty chair, and I would say, "Yeah, there's your pee-pee," and so on and so on. And sure enough, by capturing children's attention and by labeling everything, children develop from a newborn who can do little more than sleep, eat, and drool to a two-year-old who can speak hundreds of words in a given language.

Does that sound like how we use gender? It should. We capture children's attention because we "use gender" for almost every purchase we make. My kids are never more focused on their environment than when we walk into a Toys "R" Us. Their sweet little eyes scan their visual field like owls stalking field mice. With laser focus, they find the section labeled "Girls." When the nice old lady passes us and compliments them by saying, "What pretty girls you have," they have just been labeled with their assumed most important characteristic, their gender. Repeat similar scenarios thousands of times throughout their first few years of life and it is not surprising they start to learn something about the importance of gender.

To return to the language example, children also go beyond simply learning words that are frequently labeled. Children around age two also understand the basic rules of grammar and can put together simple words to form a bigger idea. For example, they can say "Daddy hit" to get Daddy to hit a ball and they can say "hit Daddy" when they hit Daddy on the head with a pillow while playing. Importantly, no one ever taught them this. I think I can speak for all parents when I say no one sits their child down and says, "When a noun comes before the verb, the noun is the subject that does the action. When a verb comes before a noun, it means the noun is an object to be acted upon." I know I never had that conversation with my kids! Yet, because children are detectives, they pick up patterns in our language and use them in their own unique ways.

And sometimes children make mistakes because they are discovering all of these language rules on their own. For example, it is common for children to make errors called overextensions, where they use one word to refer to a lot of different things. For example, Maya used to yell "Doggie" whenever she saw a dog, a cat, a squirrel, a wolf, and even a goat.

Children follow these same patterns with gender. As with the noun-verb conversation, we'd never sit down with our children and say, "Your gender is really, really important. It determines what activities you'll like and how you will behave. Please pay attention to how boys and girls behave and act accordingly." But children still pick up on gender differences, even the subtle clues. And, as when learning a language, children also make mistakes, like overusing gender, just as Maya overextended "Doggie." For example, when Maya was five, she stated very matter-of-factly that she needed to clean up her room because boys are messy and girls are neat and she needed to have a neater room. As she is one pile away from being featured on the TV show *Hoarders: Buried Alive*, I was in favor of the goal. But I have no idea where this bold statement about gender came from. In our house, the only boy (my husband) is, by far, the neatest person. Boys being messy isn't even a widely held stereotype. But in her mind, cleanliness was linked with gender. She was overextending what traits go along with gender, just as she had overextended what animals get labeled "Dog" several years earlier. She was a good detective, but she sometimes read too much into the clues.

## How Do You Teach Your Kids?

Think about how you teach (or taught) your young children about math, letters, and colors. You probably point them out frequently. You count the stairs as you walk them, you point out letters on signs or in books, and you label the color of their cups and bowls. This strategy works remarkably well. That is why we all seem to do it, even though we didn't all take a parenting class together. We see that it works, so we keep doing it.

Think about how this relates to gender. How often do you label it, by either words or colors? Why would teaching gender work any differently than teaching math, letters, and colors?

# WHY LABELING GENDER MATTERS

Rebecca Bigler, a professor of developmental psychology at the University of Texas at Austin, has spent much of her career showing that simply labeling a group leads children to develop stereotypes about those groups. Early in her career, she conducted an experiment with a group of elementary school teachers and their students. Half of the teachers were told to use gender to label, sort, and organize the classroom. They had a pink bulletin board for girls and a blue one for boys, each child's name card was written in either pink or blue, and children always lined up boy-girl-boy-girl. The teachers would say "The girls are doing a great job today" or "The boys are being good listeners."[1]

One important part of this experiment, though, was that teachers had to treat boys and girls equally. If boys were allowed to pass out the scissors, girls had to be allowed to pass out the glue—no favoritism or competition allowed! They also couldn't express any stereotypes. Boys were never asked to be "big and strong" and lift the desks; girls were never asked to sweep the floors. They simply had to "use gender" to sort, label, and classify. In other words, it was a typical, ordinary classroom. In comparison, the other half of the teachers ignored the gender of their students. They used individual names when referring to children and treated the classroom as a whole. There were no "What a smart girl" comments or "I need the boys to settle down" requests. Instead, they said, "Lauren, you are being a great helper" or "What a good learner you are!"

What did Bigler discover after teachers managed their classrooms like this for four weeks? Students in the gender-labeling classes developed stronger gender stereotypes than students in the individual-focused classes.

As a friend of mine recently asked me, "What does it mean for children to develop stereotypes? Does it really matter?" In Bigler's research on gender labeling, having gender stereotypes meant that students in the gender labeling classes were more likely to say that "only men" should do certain jobs. They said "only men" should be a construction worker, doctor, or president of the United States. They said "only women" should be a nurse, house cleaner, or babysitter. They also said that "only women" can be kind, gentle, and take care of children.

Pause a moment and reflect on this. This is extremely important.

After four weeks of simply hearing their gender labeled and being sorted into girl and boy groups, elementary school children, both boys and girls, were more likely to say that only men can be doctors or the president of the United States and only women can be nurturing and kind. Parents of daughters who want their children to aim high in their careers should take note. Parents of sons who want their children to be nurturing, caring fathers some day should take note.

Having a gender stereotype also means that students in the gender-labeling classes perceived less variability within each gender group. They were more likely to say that "all" of the boys acted one way or "none" of the girls acted another way. In other words, by having teachers simply focus on their gender instead of their individual characteristics, children began to overlook that there were, indeed, individual variations in how children, boys and girls, acted.

Why does this matter? For one, it is simply wrong. There is absolutely no behavior that all boys or all girls do, not one. But more importantly, if your kid is different from the norm in any little way, you as a parent don't want them to feel like a failure or a misfit. As individuals, there are lots of exceptions to every rule. If kids believe that "all boys like sports," something they are more likely to say after four weeks in the gender-labeling class, imagine what life is like for the boy who doesn't like sports and can't throw a ball (or even worse, throws a ball "like a girl"). Studies show that other kids will tease him, and his self-esteem will take a hit.[2] Through no fault of his own, simply because his peers think all boys or all girls should act a certain way, he gets treated poorly. In my mind, that is a big price to pay simply for the convenience of having pink and blue bulletin boards.

This type of either/or thinking was stronger in the gender-labeling class than in the individual-focused class, after only four weeks in a class that met from 8 a.m. to noon. That is not a lot of time. Image the effects of years of "using gender."

Also important, these conclusions about gender aren't taken from one random study. Bigler spent fifteen years of her career replicating this finding over and over and understanding why it happens—why using gender to organize and label people has such an effect on kids. As her graduate student, this was my training ground.

## IT ISN'T GENDER PER SE

Someone really paying attention should ask, "How do you know that using gender to label and sort is so important to children?" In real life, it is hard to know what about gender is so important because it so ever-present in society and is something we are biologically born with. Maybe children latch onto and stereotype based on gender because it is a biological trait that is important for later reproduction and mate selection. Maybe we are driven (by our genes, or the universe, or some higher power) to make gender an important part of who we are and how we think.

Carefully designed research studies have helped us figure out this issue. In a series of studies spanning a decade, we found that we could get children to form stereotypes about each other just like they do with gender. Amazingly, children do this even when we totally make up the stereotyped groups. For example, while working with Bigler in graduate school, I would give elementary school children either a blue T-shirt or a red T-shirt to wear throughout the school day for six weeks. We created these fake blue and red groups by blindly drawing names from a hat, where half of the kids were randomly assigned to the blue group and half to the red group. Teachers treated those color groups in the same ways they would use gender. Teachers said, "Good morning, blue and red kids!," "Let's line up blue, red, blue, red." Kids had their names on either a red or blue bulletin board and had either a red or blue name card on their desk. But again, teachers had to treat both groups equally and not allow them to compete with one another. They simply "used" color in the same way many teachers "use gender."[3]

What happened? After only four weeks, children formed stereotypes about their color groups. They liked their own group better than the other group. Red-shirted children would say, "Those blue-shirt kids are not as smart as the red-shirt kids." Just like they do with gender, they said that "all blue kids" act one way and "no red kids" act another way (this differed based on which group they were in). They began to segregate themselves, playing with kids from their own color group more than with those from the other group.

They were also more willing to help kids in their own color groups. Children walked into a classroom in which we had staged two partially completed puzzles. We had surreptitiously draped a red shirt across one puzzle and a blue shirt across the other. When given the option, children were more likely to help out the child they thought was in their group.

Later studies showed children as young as preschool latched on to whatever categories adults used, even groups we made up based on colored T-shirts, and formed attitudes about each other based on their group.[4, 5]

In all of these studies, there was always a very important control group. The classes where students wore colored T-shirts but the teachers didn't talk about the color groups. They didn't sort by color or use the color grouping to label each child. In other words, it was like being in a class of boys and girls where teachers don't mention or sort by gender; they simply treated them like individuals. In these classes, children didn't form stereotypes and biased attitudes about groups. If the adults ignored the groups, even when there were very visible differences, children ignored the groups, too.

So what does all of this really mean? The importance of this series of studies, and why they are a staple in most developmental psychology textbooks, is that these colored-shirt groups are completely meaningless. There is no socialization on television, no parental messages about the groups, and definitely no innate or hormonal differences that drive us to associate with only red or blue T-shirt kids. It wasn't akin to the old assumption that boys like boys and girls like girls because they are born that way. The answer is definitely not in our biology!

Instead, it seems that children pay attention to the groups that adults treat as important. When we repeatedly say, "Look at those girls playing!" or "Who is that boy with the blue hat?," children assume that being a boy or girl must be a really important feature about that person. In fact, it must be the single most important feature of that person. Otherwise, why would we point it out all the time?

## Reflection

Imagine as an adult only being able to wear one color:
>   Your room is that color.
>   Your office is that color.
>   Your car is that color.
>   Your clothes, hats, shoes, and coat are that color.
>   Your briefcase and laptop cover are that color.
>   Your cell phone case is that color.
>   Every present you get comes in that color.

It would definitely make a statement, wouldn't it? It makes a statement for kids as well.

If children see a difference, they look to experts in the world (us grown-ups) to see whether the difference is important or not. Don't forget that they see plenty of differences in people. For example, they see differences in hair color. We come in brown hair, black hair, blond hair, red hair, and gray hair. But no adult ever labels this visible category, saying, "Look at that brown-haired kid." "Okay, all the brown-haired kids and black-haired kids over here. All the red- and blond-haired kids over there." Children ultimately learn to ignore these as meaningful categories, but they still notice they exist. If I ask someone's hair color, a child can tell me. It just isn't a meaningful category. They don't develop attitudes about what it means to have red hair or brown hair (even the occasional blond joke isn't constant enough for children to notice).

But with gender, children notice the difference and adults make it meaningful. Children see the category. We made sure of that with our taped-on bows. Also, the experts in the world, their parents, always label the category. We put a figurative flashing neon arrow on gender and say, "Pay Attention! Important Information Here!" Just as with the language example, we point out, label, and repeat things we want kids to learn. And guess what? They learn them.

| Adults make the category "gender" really important. | > | Kids notice whatever adults make meaningful. | > | Kids try to understand this important category. | > | Kids develop their own explanations for gender groups.* |
|---|---|---|---|---|---|---|

*You might be surprised by these explanations!

First, children notice what adults point out as important. Second, they work really hard at coming up with explanations for the world: if being a boy or a girl is an important feature of a person, children want an explanation for why it is meaningful.

## COWS WILL BE COWS

In a cleverly titled research paper, "Boys Will Be Boys; Cows Will Be Cows," Marianne Taylor, Marjorie Rhodes, and Susan Gelman, researchers in psychology at the University of Michigan, describe their research in which they asked five- and six-year-old children about the characteristics of gender groups and animal species groups. They asked children what would happen if a cow was adopted at birth by a group of pigs. They wanted to know if children thought the cow raised by pigs would grow up mooing or oinking. They also asked children what would happen if a baby girl was adopted at birth by her uncle, who happened to live on an island inhabited only by men and boys. Would she, when she grew bigger, like to sew and play with tea sets, or would she enjoy building things and fishing (activities she was raised to do)? In other words, the researchers wanted to know if children thought girls were born with a girl "essence" (including taking care of babies, sewing, and putting on makeup) and boys were born with a boy "essence" (including playing with trucks, building things, and wanting to be a firefighter) as core traits that would exist even if the child never had any exposure to those things.[6]

Not surprising to the researchers, they found that children assume cows always moo, even among their adopted family of pigs. This is actually an accurate assumption, as cows and pigs are fundamentally different species. Cows are born with innate and unchangeable characteristics that make them moo (and not oink), and pigs are born with a different set of innate and unchangeable characteristics that make them oink (and not moo). Children understood that there was an underlying "essence" that the animals were born with that couldn't be changed or altered, no matter what they were exposed to or what they were taught.

Here's where children's assumptions about innate differences err. Children also assume that girls always play with makeup and tea sets and boys always collect baseball cards and play with fire trucks, even if the girls and boys were never exposed to these things. A cow can't do pig things, just like a girl can't do boy things and a boy can't do girl things. Children, based on the findings in this study, assume that girls are born with innate and unchangeable characteristics that fundamentally differ from the innate and unchangeable characteristics that boys are born with. No amount of exposure or teaching can change our traits and interests. In other words, boys and girls are as different as cows and pigs.

This is an important study because it points out how rigid children's thinking is when it comes to gender differences. It is similar to the old saying "Give him an inch and he will take a mile." Give kids a little push toward focusing on gender differences (and, in fact, we are giving them a massive push with our constant use of gender), and they will run with it—making us entirely different species in the process.

## ONLY BOYS CAN BE FIREMEN

Our constant labeling of gender influences children in other ways, too. Research has shown that when children hear the labels *policeman* or *fireman*, they assume only men can perform the job. When children hear the word *he* used as a generic term, they assume it refers only to boys.[7] These are hard habits of speech to break. Mothers do this a lot; I catch myself doing this regularly. In research studies where moms look at animal picture books with their young children, they refer to 95 percent of the gender-neutral animals as "he."[8] Children notice this and assume most animals are boys. (Granted, this isn't just because of moms. In children's books, boy animals outnumber girl animals 5 to 1.[9])

This use of gender in our language matters because if girls think a job, trait, or skill is only for boys, then they are less likely to want to do it. In other words, simply by labeling a firefighter a "fireman" makes girls less likely to want the job. Some may shrug because they don't really want their daughters to be firefighters anyway. But I would hate for my daughters to shy away from jobs like "chairman of the board" just because the label didn't match their own gender.

## STEREOTYPES SET IN STONE

Does it really matter whether children think all girls like to sew and all boys like to collect baseball cards? We know that with increased labeling of gender, our tendency to think that all boys have one set of attributes and all girls have another increases. But does that matter when we are raising our own kids? Yes, because once these stereotypes kick in for a child, they are extremely hard to change.

People, children included, have a strong drive to remember information that is consistent with what they know, or think they know (we come back to this in the next chapter). This drive is likely hardwired into us. We like to make predictions about the world. It helps us navigate a sometimes scary environment. I like knowing that all dogs bark, all cats meow, and all lions roar. It helps me know how to interact with a new dog or cat, and helps me remember to avoid interacting with lions. On the flip side, I would be pretty freaked out if my dog started to purr.

In the same way, the world becomes a more dependable place when I can predict how "all" boys or "all" girls will act. The problem is that all boys don't act the same, nor do all girls. Therefore, to keep our stereotypes (that is to say, predictions) intact, we have to do some fancy mental tricks.

To help us believe that our predictions are always accurate, we are good at forgetting exceptions to our rules or distorting those rules in our mind. Researchers have shown children a picture of a man standing in front of a stove while telling them that the man likes to cook dinner for his family. When children were asked about this man later, they didn't alter their stereotype about women cooking. Instead, they misremembered the story character as a woman or remembered the man as repairing the stove instead of cooking. Some children, when they were shown a picture of a female school principal, later remembered her as the "lunch lady" or secretary. Similarly, some children remembered the male cook at a hospital as a doctor—a nice promotion for him.[10]

Schools, in a noble effort to interest more girls in math and science, often try to combat stereotypes by showing children images of famous female scientists. "See, they did it. You can do it, too!" Unfortunately, these attempts rarely work, according to the research. Girls are more likely to remember the women as lab assistants. This is frustrating for those of us who try to combat gender stereotypes in children. I have spent years of my career trying to do this in schools, often failing, because our brains are too good at filtering out information that doesn't fit our preconceived notions.

Because stereotypes are so difficult to change, I always encourage parents to start at birth. You really only have about three years of heavy influence. After that, the stereotypes are ingrained in our children's minds, and the best thing we can do is address them head-on. The next best option is to help children recognize a gender stereotype when they see one, in themselves and others.

## BRINGING SCIENCE HOME

These findings are so ingrained in me that I almost never use the words *boy* or *girl* to label people; I just use the words *kids* or *grown-ups*. Instead of saying, "What a big girl you are!" to Grace, I say, "What a big kid you are!" I want to emphasize her growing independence, not her gender. The sentiment is the same, and it takes very little effort to make the shift. I even talk about my kids collectively as "the kids" (or at times "the rugrats," or on a bad day "the lunatics"), rather than "the girls." When I point them out to other people, I remark, "Look at those kids playing." Or I emphasize roles. For example, when I'm with the kids and see a family, I don't refer to the "man" or "woman"; I refer to them as "daddies" or "mommies." The "mail carrier" delivers our mail, the "garbage collector" comes every Friday, and anyone who serves us food at restaurants are "waiters." These are small language changes to make. Kids pay attention to language (it's how they learned language). Most people probably don't even notice I make small shifts in my word choices.

This usually works pretty easily, except when I'm reading books. I can still hear my husband (who typically goes along with my approach) laugh out loud when he overheard me read to our then three-year-old, "Little Kid Blue, come blow your horn, the sheep's in the meadow, the cow's in the corn." Just recently, I struggled while reading the *Boxcar Children* with Maya to find a gender-neutral word for handyman and settled on repairperson. In Grace's book about Corduroy the bear, it is not that difficult to change "saleslady" to "sales clerk" and "nightwatchman" to "security guard." And because almost all animals in children's books are labeled "he," when we read books about dinosaurs cleaning their rooms and counting to ten, I randomly change the gender of the dinosaurs back and forth. One reason I am secretly partial to *Blue's Clues* is that Blue is actually a girl and referred to as "she," a novelty in the world of children's entertainment.

My own language is pretty easy to change. Yours is, too. You probably say curse words when there are only adults around. It is pretty easy to edit yourself in front of your kids because no one wants to hear that their kid said "This is bullshit" to the teacher passing out the homework. The shame of hearing our kids repeat our words motivates us to monitor our language. Editing out gender-based terminology is no different. *Boys* and *girls* are not terrible words, but they represent categories I don't want my kids to focus on. I refer to gender when it is needed (our recent conversation about puberty being a vivid example), but often it isn't really relevant. Kids, kiddos, toddlers, babies, big kids, teenagers, people, mommies, teachers, construction workers, drivers, soccer players, runners, softball players, students, third graders, hooligans, that person in orange—they all work well as descriptions and give my kids a lot more information about someone than simply gender.

I also try to eliminate the use of gender in other ways. We do not have girls-only parties, for example. I also correct any gendered comments I hear my own kids say. When Maya made the comment that boys were messy and girls were clean, I pointed out that some boys are messy but some boys are neat (like her dad). I also pointed out that some girls are clean but some girls are messy (like her, I said with a smile). When Grace comments "Big girl!" about herself (a phrase I think she picked up at school), I repeat back, "You're right, you are a big kid!" She then repeats back (because she repeats everything we say), "Big kid!"

But the outside world is a powerful force. Both of my kids are, as are yours, constantly reminded about the importance of gender. We held Maya's eighth birthday party at a cooking school. The kids got to make their own pizza and decorate cupcakes. Because she is friends with both, there were an even number of boys and girls there. I assumed, "What a nice, stereotype-free party." I didn't realize I was about to be ambushed by the very people who took my money. The cooking instructors who led the party constantly made gendered comments. I counted ten comments in a four-minute period. Lots of "Oh, the boys are usually really wild," "The boys are actually cooking," "Boys usually throw the dough," and "Boys always like pepperoni." I wanted to shout, "I get it! All boys, without exception, because of their Y chromosome, like to make a mess with spicy meat. Call the medical journals, rewrite the Human Genome Project."

But, I thought better of it. I didn't say anything. My husband suggested I sit down for a second and take a deep breath. The party continued to drive my anti-gender-stereotype brain a little crazy. Several of the boys refused to frost their cupcakes with the strawberry frosting because it was pink. Of course, the instructors played right into that. But Maya's party wasn't the place to make the scene I desperately wanted to make.

That doesn't mean I let it drop. I can't control what other people say and I believe in being polite. When we got home, I asked Maya if she remembered what the instructors were saying at her party about boys and girls. She did. I reminded her that just because an adult says something doesn't mean it is always true. I stated, "Some adults think that all boys act one way and all girls act another way. But we know that isn't true. There is nothing that all boys do and all girls do. Some boys are wild and some girls are wild. Some boys are calm and some girls are calm."

I went further to say, "One thing I think is great about you is that you have friends who are girls and friends who are boys. I like that you are just Maya, and you don't like things just because they are supposed to be 'girl things' and dislike things just because they are supposed to be 'boy things.' You like things that are Maya things. Sometimes that is stuff that a lot of other girls like, such as pink. Sometimes that is stuff that a lot of boys like, such as cars. I think it is way more interesting and fun to play with a big mix of toys." My goal was to counteract what the adults had been saying and to reinforce her lack of gender stereotypes using specific examples. If I can't shield her from stereotypes, at least I can help her recognize them for what they are.

So, I reduce the use of gender in my language and I address any comments my kids or others make about gender. But, I don't want Maya to be the kid forced to wear a burlap sack and go by the pronoun "it." She is a girl and is socialized by the world at large. This was most evident when we moved. I let Maya pick the paint color for her new room. She picked pink. I pick my battles. Being gender neutral isn't the goal. Going beyond a simple stereotype to be the best that she can be is the goal.

Sometimes these changes are easy; sometimes they are awkward. But I put in the effort because I know how hard it is to change these stereotypes once they take hold. They are hard to change even in my own family. My husband is a firefighter. Maya once mentioned to me that only men are firefighters. "Otherwise, why would they be called firemen?" she asked incredulously. It was a valid point. I reminded her that we knew two women who were firefighters, both of whom had been assigned to my husband's station. These weren't abstract examples in a storybook. We knew them, and we have only seen these women in fire department uniforms, so there was no room for ambiguity. But Maya somehow managed to exclude them from her bold statement about firemen. We, of course, then had to have a conversation about who could be a firefighter and how difficult it is to remember that women do a certain job when we label the job with the word "man" in it. Once that stereotype gets started, it gets perpetuated by our drive to see the world in a consistent way. And once we start paying attention to gender, it is hard to stop.

# FIVE WAYS TO MINIMIZE
# GENDER ACROSS CHILDHOOD

An important caveat: I don't follow all of these ideas all of the time. Sometimes I am successful; sometimes it is out of my control. For example, if you saw Grace on any given day, you could easily call me out and say, "She is covered in pink. Seems a wee bit hypocritical, hmm?" Well, that is true a lot of days. The reality is that her grandparents buy her a lot of clothes, which is very kind, and so she wears what she has. The flip side is that to round out her color options, I never buy her pink clothes.

Sometimes, the battle is simply not one I choose to fight that day because I have to review piano homework, get gum out of someone's hair, and the spaghetti sauce is burning. In those moments, my sole parenting goal is to get the kids fed and in bed so I can collapse on the couch in a stupor; I am less concerned with maximizing their potential. But also keep in mind, a lot of these ideas only involve a little bit of effort and then the kids take over from there. So my advice is to pick the ideas that work for you, in your life, with your partner, with your parents and in-laws, with whatever energy you have left in the day.

## For Babies

1. Don't buy everything in one color. Your daughter is still a girl, even if she has some clothes that are not pink or purple. Think bright, bold primary colors. I don't think many people would dress their sons in all pink. That is okay. But something yellow every once in a while might be nice for him. Think about your baby as an actual person. Would you wear only one color?

2. Reduce the amount of times his or her clothes are literally labeled with gender. "Daddy's Strong Boy" and "Daddy's Precious Girl" bibs make gender very important from the start.

3. Make sure you talk to sons as much as to daughters. Often infant boys are talked to less often than infant girls.[11] When you are

talking, use plenty of "emotion" words with infant sons. Statements such as "Good morning! You seem happy" or "I can tell you are frustrated" help children learn about emotions and recognize them in themselves. Boys typically hear these kind of statements less often than girls do (and then as adults, we complain that men aren't "in touch with their emotions"). One day, your son's significant other will reap the benefits.

4. Read plenty of books to infant daughters about trucks and trains. All children enjoy things with wheels; it isn't coded on the Y chromosome.

5. Both boys and girls should have soft cuddly dolls. Caretaking, nurturance, and perspective taking are good traits to reinforce in all children. Girls are not the only ones who will become parents one day.

## For Toddlers

1. Buy both sons and daughters dolls, kitchen sets, trucks, and chunky Legos. All children need to be taught how to nurture and care for others and how to manipulate objects. This means crossing to the other side of Toys "R" Us. There are no trucks in the pink aisles and no dolls in the blue aisles. You are a grown-up, though. You can handle the challenge.

2. Continue to keep both types of toys in the house regardless of their use. Sons may not play much with dolls, and daughters may not play much with trucks. This may be especially true if they are around older kids who are modeling which toys belong to which group. But it will happen some. And more importantly, it says that you believe there are no such things as boy toys or girl toys.

3. Don't use gender labels when talking to your kids. They don't need to be labeled a boy or girl when you are complimenting their abilities. They will soon know their gender; that knowledge doesn't

need to be reinforced. Try substituting the word *kid* or simply use the adjective. For example, it works really well to say, "You are such a big kid," "You are so helpful," "You are such a hard worker."

4. Talk to your kids' teachers if you notice gender stereotypes at school. I am a total wuss when it comes to confrontation. I never march into a school and demand that a teacher make a change. I don't want to make the teacher defensive or uncomfortable, and I would feel I was being rude. But that doesn't mean I let it slide either. For example, I have noticed outdated books (the ones that say, "What do boys do? They can be doctors. What do girls do? They can be nurses") or a heavy emphasis on Disney princesses. My very passive-aggressive technique is to say, "You know, I know some of these books are older, and some of the messages are a bit outdated. I got these books on sale (and here I produce a handful of newer, nonstereotype-driven books), and I wonder if I could swap them out for some of the older books in the collection?"

5. Count with your daughters. Parents of young sons talk about numbers three times as much as parents of daughters do.[12] So, count everything. We have fourteen stairs in our house; I know this because we always count them. Grace knows when she eats "six grapes" and we point out the "three dogs." This helps both boys and girls be more comfortable with math concepts later on.

## For Elementary School Kids

1. Avoid reinforcing gender segregation. Have birthday parties for all of your child's friends, not just the boys or girls.

2. Have discussions with your children when they state a gender stereotype. Ask them why they think that. It is usually based on their own creative logic. For example, my friend's daughter hates oysters. She stated that because she hates oysters, only boys like oysters. When your kids make these kinds of statements,

point out that not all boys or all girls do anything. Identify and name the exceptions to the stereotype.

3. Once you are in private, discuss with your child any gender stereotypes conveyed by someone else. You may have to explain that sometimes adults make mistakes or are simply wrong. I have had this conversation several times. I tread lightly because I want my kids to be respectful of adults. But, as adults, we know that adults are sometimes misguided. The typical conversation goes like this: "You know how John's mom said she bought you that cookbook because all girls like to cook? First, I am really glad you said 'thank you.' But I also want you to know that not all girls like to cook. Some girls do and some girls don't. Plus plenty of boys like to cook, too. It doesn't matter about being a boy or girl. Some people like cooking and some people don't."

4. A lot of television for kids in elementary school aims for that "tween" demographic of ten to thirteen years old. This seems to translate into messages about sexuality for girls and about violence for boys. For example, there are a lot of shows about teenage girls trying to gain the attention of teenage boys. I frequently tell Maya, "That show is a teenager show. We need to find something else to watch." Just being on a supposed "kid's channel" (I'm looking at you, Mouse Ears) doesn't make a show appropriate for kids. Similarly, a lot of media aimed at boys is graphically and dramatically violent. This plays into the stereotype that boys should be aggressive (a stereotype exacerbated by the popularity of guns and fighting toys). Again, you need to monitor—and often censor—your child's media diet. In the same way that you don't let your child eat Twinkies before dinner, don't let your child consume media that reinforces stereotypes.

5. This is also the age when boys and girls are beginning to be "sexualized" by advertisers and retailers. Girls are valued for being pretty and wearing "teen" clothes such as short shorts

and belly-bearing tops. Boys often try to act like they have lots of girlfriends. It is okay to censor what your kids can wear. They should not "dress sexy" in elementary school. If you overhear your son talking about girls in a sexual way, it is appropriate to tell him that it is not okay to talk about girls that way.

## For Teenagers

1. In adolescence, gender takes on renewed importance, particularly as sexual interests take over. Be aware that girls feel pressure, from both media and peers, to be sexual objects who are pretty and compliant. Boys feel pressure to sexually pursue (or at least talk about sexually pursuing) those girls. Talk to your teens about this pressure. Help them label these pressures as stereotypes.

2. Teens make choices in school that can have long-term implications, and these choices shouldn't be based on stereotypes. Don't let daughters opt out of advanced math classes or boys opt out of creative writing. They may secretly like these classes but feel uncomfortable taking atypical classes.

3. Help your adolescents stay true to themselves. Help them be unique individuals. Wanting to conform is a powerful drive for teens, but it doesn't help them maximize their unique strengths.

4. Empower them to notice gender stereotypes in daily life and talk about how to combat those stereotypes. For example, it is interesting to talk about why so few people cheer on the high school girl players at basketball games but do cheer on the boys.

5. Empower them to notice gender stereotypes in society at large and then try to take action. A conversation about the lack of female presidents, and the complex reasons for the power imbalance, is appropriate and helpful.

# THE FINAL FOUR:
## WHAT ARE THE KEY ISSUES?

- Just as when learning a language, children rely on subtle cues from adults to learn about the world. Constant use of gender to label and sort children matters; children use this information from adults to figure out what is important in the world.

- Just seeing two groups, like boys and girls, does not make children develop stereotypes; children assume that, even though the groups are visibly different, they are not meaningfully different. However, with gender, adults make these groupings meaningful.

- Once children learn that being a boy or a girl is important, they come up with their own, often inaccurate, explanations about how boys and girls differ. They assume boys and girls are different in deep, fundamental ways. They assume that culturally specific traits, like wanting to sew or be a firefighter, are innate and biologically driven. They may also overextend the use of gender to any trait that is or is not like themselves (such as enjoying oysters).

- Once these stereotypes are in place, they are difficult to change. You only have about three years of solid influence. Then the outside world trickles in, and you will need to confront the stereotypes head-on.

# Why We Focus on Gender Differences

**I am frequently asked what I do for work**—you know, the standard airplane, cocktail party, just-met-your-new-neighbor small-talk opening line. I usually say "professor," having learned that saying "psychologist" always results in a joke about whether I need a case study. But these conversations inevitably lead me to explain that I study gender stereotypes. This is usually followed by my new pal saying something like, "But boys and girls really are different. Of course, we treat boys and girls differently (eye roll); it is just pointing out the obvious. It is unavoidable." This may be true, but for different reasons than you may think.

Maybe we will always point out, label, and categorize by gender. Maybe everything I have described so far in this book is inevitable and unavoidable. But that isn't necessarily because boys and girls are so different from one another. More likely, we cling to this obsession with gender because we love to categorize people, regardless of the criteria.

Why do we label and sort by gender all the time? We like to think we have this focus because it is an important biological grouping that tells us a lot about people. For example, knowing that my friend has a daughter, I assume I'll have a leg up in picking out a toy she would like at Toys "R" Us. But, in reality, we sort on the basis of anything if given the chance.

In this chapter, I describe the research showing that we are born to categorize people, no matter what the group. As you will see, we are pretty lazy thinkers when it comes to people, and categories make it easy to be lazy. The cost of this laziness is that we make a lot of errors in how we think about people, and it's unfortunate when the errors affect our kids.

## WE ARE BORN SORTERS

We have a couple of fundamental abilities from birth. Unless something goes really wrong in development, all babies around the world, regardless of whether they grow up in a Manhattan high-rise or an African village, quickly learn how to categorize. With little input from adults, and only a small bit of exposure, babies can categorize all sorts of stuff. Babies come out of the womb inundated with perceptual information—different sights, sounds, textures, movements. They innately begin looking for correlations among all that information, seemingly designed from birth to figure out how the details go together.

Take two animals, dogs and bears. Infants quickly learn these are two different categories, even though there are similarities between them. Both have fur, four legs, mouths, eyes, and ears. But the smaller animals always bark, and the larger animals always roar. Babies can pick up on these correlations (between size and sound) and learn that the animals belong to two different groups. Babies can learn categories like these long before they can talk—even before they can sit up. Grace's preschool friends amazed me the other day. They were correctly naming very abstract pictures of animals in a watercolor painting. They were able to detect the shape of a trunk and know it was an elephant and could detect the stripes of a tiger. They knew enough about some key characteristics to figure out the category, even when major details (like the actual bodies) were missing.

This ability to form categories, whether of animals, cars, or food, is important for babies. It helps them navigate a really complicated world early on. The quicker a baby can group information, the quicker that baby can get what it needs or move on to learning about the next thing. The quicker babies learn that apples, pears, and plums are all sweet fruits that they enjoy—and that tomatoes don't belong to that group—the happier they are.

Poor Grace has struggled with this one. We eat a lot of grape tomatoes in our salads and she enthusiastically eats one every time, shouting "Grape!" She loves grapes and eats them by the handful. Every time, though, she spits out the tomato in disgust. She has traumatized herself, at least based on her overly dramatic reaction, because those tomatoes pretend to be in one category but really belong to another one. It rocks her world every week. But her shocked reaction to this one exception shows how good we usually are at forming categories, and how we are usually right. This is one of our most adaptive qualities for surviving as humans.

## NOTHING IS AS FUN AS A FACE

A second fundamental ability humans are born with, in addition to forming categories, is the universal capacity to pay attention to and learn about faces. Within hours, as soon as the nurse wipes the gunk off your baby's eyes, he or she shows a preference for faces over anything and everything else. Of all the innate tendencies we have as humans, zeroing in on people is a really important one. People are the ones most likely to feed us and protect us from danger. It always pays off to pay attention to the gravy train. And those pregnancy pains were worth it, because within the first week, newborns prefer mom's face to a stranger's face. It is a complex mix of familiarity, early love, and recognizing their meal ticket.

(A side note on research with babies: Most research has focused on moms instead of dads, as moms have historically been what researchers call the "primary caregiver." Times are definitely changing, and many dads are raising babies by themselves or with another dad. But the numbers of those dads is still relatively small, and researchers are slow to catch up. The result is that we know a lot more about how babies look at moms than at dads. Even among babies with a mom and a dad at home, the majority of babies spend most of their early days with mom, especially if they are nursing.)

Babies are adept at learning about faces. Before they can roll over, around three months old, they can distinguish other people's faces, especially those of women who are the same race as their mom (because this is the person category they see the most frequently). Even with shoddy vision, they are already becoming experts about their most familiar category.

By six months old, babies recognize that women's faces and men's faces belong to two different categories. When researchers show babies a series of pictures of women, babies are interested and stare intently at the pictures. But when the researchers keep showing one picture after another of many different women, babies eventually become bored. It is as though they said, "We get it. Women. Move on." They finally turn away, uninterested by the repetition of the same category. If the researchers then show the six-month-old babies a picture of a man, they become interested again. They recognize that the researchers have finally showed them something new. They now start looking at the pictures again, recognizing that the new pictures belong to a new category.[1]

They need some help, though, to see these two categories of people. We aren't born knowing men from women. To help babies recognize that men and women are different, they need the hair cues (women with short hair can throw them off), and they need delicate features for women and strong jaws for men.[2] Everyone needs to be a classic stereotype of their category. Men are actually pretty tricky to sort. Their characteristics differ a lot from each other. Ryan Gosling, with his more delicate features, and Russell Crowe, with his square jaw and scruffy beard, have drastically different characteristics, and it is difficult for babies to pick up on the common details of men to put them into one group. In other words, when there is a lot of variability in people who belong to one group, babies have a harder time forming the category.

Over the next year, babies get better at sorting people into gender groups. By their first birthday, babies can match female voices to female faces and male voices to male faces. They actually look longer at the face that matches the gender of the voice they are hearing. They pick up on the link that all of those people with long hair also have high-pitched voices. By sixteen months, babies can label the gender of their parents. Then they are off to the races. Labeling categories helps sorting, and by two years old, kids are experts.

We don't just sort by gender, though. We are born with those two strong drives: to categorize everything and to focus on people. It is only logical that we are going to use our sorting powers on our favorite subject, people. And sort them we do, regardless of the grouping.

## LATCHING ON TO ANY GROUP

When Hersz Mordche was born to Jewish parents in Poland in 1919, his future was pretty uncertain. At the time, anti-Semitism was rampant and Polish Jews weren't allowed to have much of an education. When it was time for advanced studies, Mordche left Poland and traveled to France to study chemistry at the Sorbonne. Not long after, as World War II began, he left his studies to help the French army fight Hitler. A year later he was captured by the Germans and held as a prisoner of war. Mordche, who now called himself Henri Tajfel, knew the importance of belonging to the "right" group. He admitted to his German captors that he was Jewish but claimed to be a French citizen, knowing that a Polish Jew would certainly be executed. When he was finally released from captivity, he discovered that his entire family and most of his friends in Poland had died in the Holocaust. He was overwhelmed with the realization that so many Germans, seemingly normal and decent people, had developed such a hatred of Jews that they had been complicit in their deaths. With this realization, he was no longer interested in chemistry. Instead, he embarked on a career in psychology to better understand why and how one group of people could form such hostility toward another group of people. What he discovered was that it doesn't take much.[3]

Tajfel, who went on to become a social psychologist at Bristol University in England, pioneered what came to be known as the minimal group experiment. He found that simply putting people into a group, regardless of whether the group was meaningful or not, led to stereotyping and prejudice. In one of his now classic studies, he showed research participants two paintings, one by Paul Klee and one by Wassily Kandinsky, and asked them which they preferred. Regardless of their answer, he told them he was assigning them to a group with other people who had the same tastes. Sometimes he labeled the newly formed groups as the "Klee group" and the "Kandinsky group," and sometimes he never gave the group a label. When people thought they belonged to the "Klee group," they thought their group was best. Likewise, people who belonged to the group labeled "Kandinsky group" thought their group was best. However, if the researchers didn't label these groups, people didn't really care and liked both groups just the same.[4]

Tajfel took it a step further, though. He randomly divided some new research participants into an "X" group and "W" group. He simply tossed a coin. And the participants knew they were assigned to a group based on a coin toss. Again, as in the Klee and Kandinsky study, he sometimes labeled the group "X" or "W" and sometimes he didn't. He found that, even when the groups were random, even when people knew the groups were random and based on a coin toss, they were biased toward their group when their group was labeled. Thousands of studies have since reaffirmed that people almost always do this when put into groups. Psychologists have gotten research participants to form stereotypes on the basis of whether they are wearing a red or blue shirt, whether they are assigned to one summer camp cabin or another, and even whether they think they overestimate or underestimate the number of dots on a chalkboard. Simply putting people into groups—even totally meaningless groups based on coin tosses—leads them to latch on to these groups and form attitudes related to the groups.

This doesn't just happen in a research lab. In real life, we also do this with any kind of group. I'm a professor at the University of Kentucky, a school with an excellent basketball team. My students get riled up when asked what they think of Duke, another basketball powerhouse. Or ask Yankees fans what they think of the Red Sox. There is a rivalry between cops and firefighters in many cities (popular T-shirts proclaim, "If you can't take the heat, become a cop" or "If you can't walk the beat, become a firefighter"). Or ask *Twilight* fans whether they are Team Edward or Team Jacob.

The groups we like to latch on to can be more meaningful than who shoots a ball best. Ask Republicans what they think of Democrats and vice versa. The hatred of the "other" party and the strong partisanship of modern politics made the 112th Congress the least productive Congress since World War II.[5] I would say, ask African-Americans what they think of whites and whites what they think of African-Americans, but we have learned to hide our true feelings when it comes to race. When we measure people's attitudes without them knowing it, by measuring their "implicit attitudes," we see that these groups are just as meaningful as ever, with each group liking their own group best. Think racial stereotypes are long gone? Google "racist jokes and Obama." They're not gone . . . by a long shot.

Want to see some hard-core ramifications of the groups we latch on to? Ask Israelis what they think of Palestinians and vice versa. These groups are just as important for children as for adults. Daniel Bar-Tal, a Jewish Israeli psychologist at Tel-Aviv University, reports research showing that the vast majority of Israeli children in elementary school associated Palestinians with "violent acts such as kidnapping, murder, terrorism, and criminality."[6] These attitudes aren't based on children's actual experience and exist even if children live in areas with no nearby conflict. When children are shown a picture of a person who could be either Jewish or Arab, simply based on whether his name fits one group or the other, children describe the man as either friendly or mean: same man, same expression; only the group has changed.

Obviously, the Israeli and Palestinian conflict is much more complicated than the Yankees versus Red Sox rivalry, but the human tendency to sort, categorize, and judge on the basis of those categories drives it all—and is present from birth.

## WHY WE LOVE A CATEGORY

We likely have a biological tendency to use categories and form stereotypes based on those categories. After all, the world is highly complex. We encounter new people and have new experiences every minute. Even a boring day is full of new sights and sounds, if you pay attention. As humans, we have evolved and adapted to sort and categorize all we encounter in this complex world.

That skill has served us well. It's helpful to know that bears are dangerous. I don't need to evaluate the individual characteristics of the bear; I can lump them into one group and quickly get the hell out of the forest. In our evolutionary past, it was likely beneficial to know which group a person belonged to as a quick way to distinguish friends from enemies. It made adaptive sense to make these quick decisions.

Our modern world is more highly complex than ever. Walking into Toys "R" Us would make our ancestors flee in fear. (I often have that urge myself.) Being able to divide Toys "R" Us in half and only shop the girl half or the boy half makes life much quicker and easier. The Toys "R" Us flagship store in Times Square is 110,000 square feet of chaos.

If I can shave an hour off my shopping trip, I am more likely to survive.

More than anything else, though, we are lazy—maybe lazy with good reasons, but lazy nonetheless. Susan Fiske and Shelly Taylor wrote an influential book about social cognition based on their work as social psychologists at Harvard. In it, they coined a term that has stuck because it explains a lot of human behavior. They describe humans as cognitive misers.[7] Just as Ebenezer Scrooge wouldn't spend a penny unless he had to, we don't spend any mental energy unless absolutely necessary.

Instead, individuals rely on simple and efficient ways of processing new information and making judgments. It takes too much mental effort to fully evaluate every new piece of information that comes our way. If we did, we'd have information overload. Imagine the new parent who stumbles into the bottle section at a baby superstore and is trying to pick out the best type of bottle—one reduces colic, one has the safest plastic, one is dishwasher safe, one is latex free, one best mimics mom. All of this competing information leads to paralysis. A person could stand in the aisle for hours reading labels. Instead, we have to quickly categorize things and move on. We don't have time to be rational and objectively think about every possible detail. We would be paralyzed by every new situation. It is much more efficient for this parent to think, "This label looks familiar; the commercial was just on. I will just get this one."

The categories in our minds are well established—we have been creating them since birth, so it doesn't take much mental energy to store new information. It also means we don't pay much attention to new information. We force it into a bin whether it fits perfectly or not. Our minds work like a well-organized playroom. There are bins for everything: cars, puzzles, crayons, farm animals. It took a long time to get it organized, but once everything has a container, it is easy to keep clean. Even young kids can learn to quickly put away their toys in the right bin. They find a car between couch cushions. Quick, toss it into the car box. Find some random crayons lying around? The kids know where they go. Without this sorting system, the place would stay a cluttered mess. Okay, if you can actually get your kids to do this, please give me a call and tell me how. But the metaphor works. We have categories in our minds that help us organize and process our worlds. We use those categories because it is an easier and more efficient way to navigate life than to attend to every individual characteristic.

In our everyday lives, it is often useful to be "cognitive misers." It is helpful to have quick, organized categories to use in a pinch. My own daily experiences as a mom highlight this usefulness (even though I work incredibly hard to fight the categories). For example, in any given school year, Maya is invited to up to ten birthday parties. I only vaguely know most of these kids. I may recognize them from school, but I definitely don't know what kind of toys they might like. So party time comes, and we need a last-minute gift. If I can run into the store and pick up something quickly, between piano lessons and the softball game, it makes my life easier. That is my modern version of a quick decision. Instead of paying attention to the individual characteristics of the birthday child, my human (overwhelmed) brain quickly goes to what I think an average eight-year-old girl might like. Five minutes in and out, present wrapped in the car, and we arrive at the party only five minutes late. Trying to be quick and easy often leads to a heavy reliance on stereotypes, despite our best intentions.

## GENDER SCHMENDER

From birth, we gravitate toward grouping people. We form groups, and base our attitudes on those groups, even when they are entirely meaningless. This helps us quickly process our complex world, and is part of why humans remain at the top of the food chain. We latch on to gender as an important grouping because it is easy. It helps us reduce the individual (messy) details of a given situation.

But that really has little to do with gender. In fact, in the next two chapters, I describe how there aren't actually that many differences. We don't latch on to gender because it is an important biological distinction. There are lots of those distinctions: short and tall, brown eyes and blue eyes, white and black. And we used to sort by race all the time. We had different schools and different water fountains. That is a grouping based on physical traits that most people deem socially unacceptable. But because we love—and maybe cognitively need—a group to distinguish each other as humans, we use another one: gender. It is less about the biological origins of the group and more about the cognitive ease it provides us.

Why is gender so easily used as a category? We make it easy by highlighting it every chance we get. Every pink or blue T-shirt, every taped-on bow, every "Good morning, boys and girls," every "Boys will be boys" comment strengthens the category and makes it more accessible. Neuroscience has shown us that the more we hear, see, or think about something, the more those neural pathways strengthen and the easier it is to keep taking that path. When we quickly need to sort the world, gender categories are ready to be pulled out.

## WHAT HAPPENS WHEN WE GROUP PEOPLE?

This innate drive to use groups is helpful when we are talking about bears and tomatoes. But when it comes to sorting people, we have a few glitches in the system. We sometimes make errors (like Grace did with those confusing grape tomatoes)—often we make the same types of errors over and over. The errors aren't random, either.

The errors we make serve an important purpose. Our brains are happiest when everything is consistent. But life is full of dissonance—people acting any which way they want in ways we can't predict (a lesson every parent learns the hard way in week one). To have consistency in a world full of dissonance, we do all sorts of mental tricks to make the information that comes in consistent with what we already think. We like our mental playroom to be nicely organized, but we also don't like to have to reorganize it after we've done it once. When we make the information fit, we are just strengthening those categories more and more over time.

We engage in three consistent mental tricks in our thinking when we sort people into groups.

## The First Mental Trick: Exaggerating Between-Group Differences

We exaggerate any differences between groups. We want to believe each of our category "bins" are really different, so we play up the differences between them. Tajfel, in another classic study, found that if he drew a series of lines on the board, and grouped some lines on one side and labeled them A and grouped different lines on the other side and labeled them B, then the people in his study perceived the A lines to differ in length from the B lines. The error is that the lines were the exact same length.[8] The same principle works with people. If I see a boy get a 92 on his math test and a girl get an 89 on hers, I focus on the differences between them instead of the similarities. I report that he got an A and she got a B, instead of saying their scores only differed by three points.

## The Second Mental Trick: Exaggerating Within-Group Similarities

We exaggerate the similarities of members within another group. For example, you may have heard some variation of this phrase in reference to racial groups: "They all look alike." It is hard to see that this is just an optical illusion, but it is. And everyone, regardless of his or her racial group, makes the same error.

We aren't born with this mental trick; it develops with time and experience. For example, at three months old, white infants can distinguish the individual faces of people from lots of different races—white, Middle Eastern, Asian, African-American. When they are six months old, they are getting better at forming groups based on race, but they can only distinguish individual people if they are white or Asian. By the time white babies approach nine months old, they can only see the differences among individual white faces.[9] Everyone else looks the same.

We do the same thing with other categories. When they are shown a lot of faces of cute little monkeys, babies at only six months old can remember the individual faces they have seen before and can distinguish between individual monkeys. Three months later, the monkeys all look alike to the babies.[10] I have taken this test myself. It is true: all the monkeys look alike to me. Here is a situation in which the infant outsmarts the adult. Even though we start out as small babies who can see the differences between people (or monkeys) within a given group that is not our own, the similarities we perceive later override any differences we originally could see.

Because we make our groups so distinct, so front and center, we are primed to think that girls are really similar to each other, boys are really similar to each other, and boys and girls are really different from one another. So I am much more likely to rush into Toys "R" Us for a birthday gift, assuming Maya's female friends will like whatever Maya likes, because I'm also assuming most girls are similar to my own daughter while her male friends will not like whatever she likes, because most boys are different from my daughter. It is the exact same premise behind thinking the A and B lines differ in the example above. This kind of thinking helps me be consistent and not worry about the pesky little details that come along with individuals.

## The Third Mental Trick: Remembering Stereotype-Consistent Information

We only pay attention to and remember the information that fits our way of thinking. If you think everyone is the same, then you overlook any differences. On Grace's first day of her new preschool, she clung to my leg and tentatively surveyed her surroundings. Meanwhile, a very loud and outgoing boy roared around the room. The teacher matter-of-factly stated, "Boys just bound into the room exploring, while girls are more timid and take their time." This was meant to be reassuring, but there was a tiny problem: it wasn't true. The only other boy at preschool that morning was outside the door, crying with his mom, refusing to even approach the classroom. His crying could be heard where we stood, but the teacher had overlooked the piece of evidence that didn't fit her way of thinking.

Hundreds of studies have shown that we are good at forgetting the exceptions to our rules. In one example, researchers read stories to study participants in which either a male or a female student lost a math contest. Overwhelmingly, participants forgot the details in the story that didn't fit their gender stereotype and added details that strengthened their preconceived notions. For example, 89 percent of the people in the study forgot that the male math student cried and 83 percent forgot that the female student beat a pillow in frustration. Plus, half of the study participants completely made up new information to fit their stereotype, falsely remembering the female as pouting and complaining and the male as playing violent video games.[11]

## FIGHTING THE LAZINESS

The mental tricks people play to keep their groupings intact affect your kids. This is extremely important to parents of a child who is different from the norm in any little way. And the reality is that most kids are! For example, a teacher may be unsure of how to soothe a sensitive boy who is crying if he or she don't recognize that sensitivity and heightened emotions are a normal male trait (chapter 4 describes research with male infants showing this is perfectly normal).

Your kids' unique qualities may be overlooked or simplified. If the teacher assumes that Grace is a timid, proper girl, she won't be prepared when Grace's true bold and fearless nature comes out ten minutes after arrival at school. A teacher who quickly pegs her as a "typical girl" won't be prepared for the very small child scaling the ten-foot-high jungle gym.

What is a parent to do? Sometimes, I try to delicately point out the differences between girls. I responded to Grace's teacher by saying,

"Well, my oldest daughter would attack a room right away. She walks up to everyone like she knows them." I also try to emphasize the ways in which my own daughters don't fit the stereotype while highlighting their unique qualities. I want the teacher to be aware that Grace is fearless once she is comfortable and help maximize Grace's strength instead of overlooking it. If I had a sensitive boy, I would tell the teacher how he likes to be soothed. This becomes even more important as kids age, especially if you have a computer-whiz daughter or a poetry-writing son.

I try to remember that we are all cognitive misers, finding it much easier to assume all girls are more timid than boys and overlooking exceptions that challenge our rules. But, the trouble is that the three mental tricks we use are flawed; the "exceptions" to our rules are actual kids who don't fit neatly into a category. When we ignore how they differ from others, we also ignore their unique qualities and strengths.

It is easier to lump markers, pencils, and crayons into the same playroom bin than to have separate bins for each. But if we keep doing that, over and over, our bins lose their usefulness—they don't help us find things. We will see in the next chapter that categorizing by gender has lost much of its usefulness; it blocks us from predicting our kids' strengths and vulnerabilities or maximizing their potential. The reality is that kids are complicated, far too complicated and distinct to be sorted into only one of two bins.

## THE FINAL FOUR:
## WHAT ARE THE KEY ISSUES?

- Practically from birth, we have the capacity to put anything into categories, and our favorite thing to sort is people. Categorizing helps us conserve mental energy in a really complicated world. We are lazy thinkers, but quick categorization has helped us stay at the top of the food chain.

- We form categories and stereotypes on the basis of anything, even when groupings are totally random. Don't believe me? Ask football fans what they think of their biggest rivals.

- We have such strong stereotypes about gender because it is an easy grouping to latch on to. It has nothing to do with gender per se. We are just looking for a straightforward way to simplify the world. We make gender grouping easy to do by frequently highlighting gender with every blue stroller or taped-on hair bow or "pretty girl"/ "strong boy" comment.

- Because of how we conserve mental energy, we think people in one group are more similar to each other than they really are, we think people in different groups are more different from each other than they really are, and we ignore or forget any exceptions to our rules. So when we assume girls are really similar to one another and very different from boys, it is just an illusion.

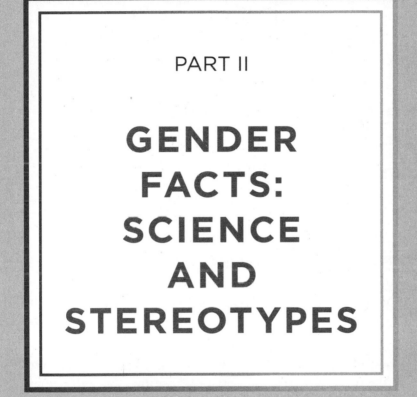

PART II

# GENDER FACTS: SCIENCE AND STEREOTYPES

## CHAPTER 4

# There Are Gender Differences

**Nietzsche once said, "There are . . . people** who, instead of solving a problem, bungle it and make it more difficult for all who come after. Whoever can't hit the nail on the head should, please, not hit at all."[1] Of the dozens of books written about gender differences, there are a lot of bad nail hits. John Gray wrote a book that sold forty million copies in forty-three languages and was named by *USA Today* as one of the twenty-five most influential books of the twentieth century.[2] *Men Are from Mars, Women Are from Venus* cemented itself in our collective conscience, with its premise of men and women being so vastly different from each other that they couldn't possibly understand one another without the help of a translator (namely, John Gray). Michael Gurian, who teaches the many ways that *Boys and Girls Learn Differently!*, is doing the same for education today.[3] Hundreds of school districts around the country teach boys and girls as if they come from two different planets (chapter 11 delves into this craziness). The problem is that these authors, the ones who claim that there are widespread differences between boys and girls, misuse and misinterpret science. They can't seem to hit the nail on the head.

It is important to understand what actual gender differences do exist and to understand where they come from. In a world obsessed with gender differences, we need to be able to separate science from assumptions, facts from fiction. Gender is so central to how we think about people, particularly children, that it is sometimes difficult to know what is real and what is simply a stereotype. Sorting that out is the goal of this chapter.

Knowing what the actual differences are (and are not) helps us as parents better recognize our individual children's strengths and weaknesses. Imagine two moms, both of whom have third-grade daughters struggling in math class. One mom chalks it up to innate differences between boys and girls in math ability and tells her daughter not to worry too much about it. She might even say, "Don't worry I wasn't very good at math either." The second mom knows that there are no meaningful gender differences in math abilities in elementary school, recognizes that her daughter has a specific problem understanding multiplication, and spends extra time going over math facts at night.

Those two girls will have very different academic experiences of math. The first daughter will continue to struggle, eventually disengage from caring about it, and become the teenage girl who claims to hate math. Her mom's early assumptions about girls and math, in fact, created the very result the mother presumed: girls dislike math. The second daughter, however, caught back up with her peers, breezed through division because of the extra help, and became a perfectly happy high school calculus student. Knowing what gender differences are, and knowing our role in shaping those differences, is key to raising children who can maximize their potential.

Much of this book discusses the ways that boys and girls are similar. But there are indeed some real differences. Some are large, some are quite small, and some start very small and get larger over time. When we put together all of the research on gender differences, the complete picture is less dramatic than a Mars-Venus mindset suggests. As Kathryn Dindia, an expert on gender differences, stated, "Instead of different planets, it is more accurate to say men are from North Dakota and women from South Dakota."[4]

# GENDER DIFFERENCES AND RESEARCH

Before we delve into where gender differences do exist, it helps to understand a couple of issues that arise when doing research on gender.

## Differentiate Between Babies and Adults

First, to really understand gender differences, especially to understand which differences are innate and which are created through experiences, it is important to recognize the distinction between research with babies and research with adults. Gender differences among men and women are very different from gender differences among infants. Both are important to understand, but for different reasons. Understanding differences between adult men and women can help enhance communication in a marriage. This is why John Gray has sold millions of books about Mars and Venus. I never make the argument that adult men and women are the same.

After ten minutes with my husband, I am often reminded of how very different we are. For example, we may have a minor argument about cleaning the dishes. He seems to remember only the times he cleans them and would likely say the same thing about me. I will be upset about the argument for the rest of the day and want to talk about it later in the evening. When I bring it up, about how my feelings were hurt but I hope I wasn't dismissive of his feelings, he will look at me with a blank stare. He wasn't bothered by the exchange and doesn't even remember that it occurred. He looks at me like I just landed from Venus. Our emotional needs, worries, and expressions are clearly different.

Seeing gender differences in adult men and women doesn't tell us anything about the ways we are innately different or anything about children. Just because women do x and men do y doesn't mean that girls do x and boys do y—or that any female must, by nature of her extra X chromosome, do x or that any male must, by nature of his Y chromosome, do y. Males and females have grown up in different worlds that have shaped behavior, mannerisms, preferences, skills, and even brain structure (chapter 6 talks more about how experiences affect the brain). For example, just because women cry more often than men does not mean that girls cry more often than boys. Practically speaking, knowing about gender differences in adults does not help a parent or teacher. To truly understand where our real differences lie, we need to examine what differences exist early in life, before stereotypes makes permanent impressions on our brains and behavior.

## Know Which Research to Believe

Relying on common sense and stereotypes as a basis for our knowledge about gender differences keeps us pretty misinformed. Listening to your mom describe the differences between you and your brother is not very informative either. To really understand where the differences are, we should be able to look to research studies. Unfortunately, there is often an assumption that research is unreliable and that anyone can find any result if they ask the right question.

A key to understanding gender differences is to know who to believe about the differences. Individual studies are sometimes hard to interpret. Maybe the researchers were "looking" for differences, or for no differences. Maybe the researchers picked a specific group of kids who were unique in some way that affected their results. Or even worse, maybe the study was a single study done with rats (which happens regularly, something we touch on in chapter 6).

Instead of relying on single studies, we should look to meta-analyses for learning about actual gender differences. A meta-analysis takes all the studies that have been done on a topic (often hundreds of them), metaphorically dumps them into one big pot, and analyzes all of the findings together.

As a way to analyze all of the possible research on a given topic, meta-analyses also include unpublished studies. To find these, the researchers email everyone who might know anyone who ever did this kind of research. Why would they want unpublished studies? It is because journals tend to publish studies that show differences between groups (for example, differences between boys and girls), and not publish studies that show no differences. The reasons for this can be pretty complex, and have a lot to do with statistical inferences (so I will spare you the lecture on hypothesis testing). Suffice it to say it is similar to why we hear about a new drug to treat cancer but never hear about the hundreds of drugs that were tried but didn't work. The end result is that studies showing no differences end up in the researcher's file drawer instead of in journals. Knowing that meta-analyses represent all research on a subject helps us be more confident in our conclusions; we know the data we're seeing aren't biased by what journals tend to publish.

Conclusions from an individual study could reflect random fluke results. Furthermore, results from studies of adults are simply capturing a difference in traits that may be the result of a lifetime of being socialized into a gender group. That is why the best way to really know what gender differences exist is to look at meta-analyses conducted with infants and children.

## WHERE THE DIFFERENCES REALLY ARE

As I have argued in part I of this book, we are obsessed with gender and gender differences. Because of this obsession, thousands and thousands of studies have been conducted to look for gender differences. In 2011, there was even a meta-analysis of 111 studies that looked solely at gender differences in nightmare frequency.[5] That means more than one hundred different studies were conducted to investigate whether the boogey-man appears more often in the dreams of boys or girls! For topics like math abilities (and others in which common sense and cultural conditioning suggest that gender differences do exist), the number of studies is even larger.

One of the most influential meta-analyses is actually a meta-analysis of forty-six different meta-analyses. In other words, millions of people were in hundreds of studies, all by different researchers, that looked for gender differences in verbal skills, math abilities, aggression, talkativeness, emotion, helping behavior, and so on, ad nauseam. Those hundreds of studies were analyzed by dozens of meta-analyses. Those dozens of meta-analyses were then analyzed in a giant meta-meta-analysis by Janet Shibley Hyde, a professor of psychology at the University of Wisconsin.[6] Hyde is an extremely well-respected researcher who studies gender differences. She has been repeatedly honored by the American Psychological Association and is listed as one of the Top 100 Psychologists Cited in Introductory Psychology Textbooks.[7] In other words, she's no hack. She has spent the past couple of decades analyzing all of the many studies conducted on gender differences. By combining all of the available research, one of her smaller research samples involved 1,286,350 people. So, her conclusions are not based on a small sample of unique children. What has she concluded after all this analysis? That boys and girls are far more similar than different.

Where exactly do gender differences exist, and where do they exist only in our imagination? In the largest and most thorough analyses to date, with the sample of more than one million people and comparisons of 124 possible gender differences, Hyde found that 78 percent of the studies found either nonexistent or very few gender differences. In other words, the vast majority of studies conducted to look for differences between males and females found, in fact, no or very few differences. This is ironic because most of these studies were looking for gender differences in those areas where we are most likely to think we are different, such as emotions, verbal skills, and math abilities.

## Temperment and Emotion

One area where researchers have long looked for gender differences is in temperament. Temperament is our biologically based emotional and behavioral reactions; they appear early in life and predict, to a large degree, our later personality. Any parent who has had more than one child knows what temperament is: it's why your first child went to sleep easily, was a good eater, didn't fuss much, and was easy to entertain at a restaurant, while your second child never napped, hated all vegetables, and threw scene-causing tantrums at Target. You parented them the same way, but they were clearly different from birth. It is why parents mutter, when their kids aren't listening, "Thank God I didn't have Jamie first. Otherwise, I would never have had another one."

Boys and girls differ in some parts of their temperament and not in other parts. For example, there are no meaningful differences in how well kids adapt to new situations or in how difficult, intense, shy, or fearful they are. Despite the stereotype, girls are not more fearful or scared of new things than boys are. The teacher who said girls are more timid than boys was simply wrong. Nor are boys more difficult or harder to control than girls. There are also no meaningful differences in their levels of anger, sadness, happiness, pleasure, or emotionality. Despite the fact that I cry every time I watch a sentimental television commercial and my husband appears to be made of stone, girls, on average, are not more emotional than boys.

This inaccurate assumption, that girls are more emotional than boys, is particularly harmful to boys. If a boy gets hurt, his first reaction usually is to cry. But this reaction is often met with the admonition that "Boys don't cry." These admonitions strike me as ridiculous. If boys don't cry, then you shouldn't have to tell your son that boys don't cry. I never have to tell my dog that dogs don't meow. She doesn't meow, will never meow, and me telling her this tidbit is pretty irrelevant. Repeatedly telling a crying boy that boys don't cry is ignoring the obvious: that boys do, in fact, cry.

What these admonitions do, besides defy logic, is teach boys that negative or sad emotions are something only girls are allowed to express. This shapes their emotion schemas, the ideas we hold about what emotions feel like, how they should be labeled, and how they should be expressed. We aren't born with these schemas; we are taught them. Boys are taught that sadness is not okay, and expressing sadness is definitely not okay, despite sadness being a normal human emotion experienced by people around the world.

We all know that emotions don't disappear; they have to come out in some way. For boys, while crying and sadness are not okay, anger is allowable. Studies have shown that mothers discuss sadness for longer and in greater detail with daughters than with sons, and discuss anger with their sons more than daughters.[8] Boys can fight and show aggression and are rarely admonished for it ("You know boys. They are always fighting …"). So boys, who grow up into men, respond to events that might cause sadness with anger instead, and we end up with adult gender differences in which women can show sadness and cry and men blow their tops.

Although boys and girls are largely similar in temperament, there are a couple of moderate differences, most notably "inhibitory control" and "surgency." In other words, boys are slightly less able to suppress inappropriate responses and slightly more exuberant than girls. Some boys have a stronger tendency to blurt out something embarrassing when company is visiting or are more likely to grab something off the shelf at the grocery store than some girls.

A common assumption is that boys are very active, while girls sit passively and play with tea sets. This assumption is pervasive, even popping up in children's books. For example, when researchers analyzed the characters in children's books, they found that boys are overwhelmingly portrayed as active and girls are overwhelmingly portrayed as passive.[9]

What does research show about boys' and girls' actual activity levels? Beyond the differences in inhibitory control and surgency, there are only minuscule differences in activity levels from infancy. Baby boys and girls don't differ much in their wiggliness. That difference becomes more pronounced in older children, and by elementary school, older boys are more inclined than girls to run, jump, and wrestle.[10] What starts as a small to nonexistent difference becomes larger across childhood, a pattern that gets repeated for other traits as well. We shouldn't be surprised that differences develop when children are being socialized in accordance with stereotypes (for example, by reading those stereotypical story books). Part III delves further into how we are able to create these differences over the course of childhood.

## Reflection

Think about what behaviors you attribute to gender. Do you use gender to explain your son's aggression ("You know how boys are, always getting in a tussle")? Do you use gender to explain why your daughter cries ("Girls and their emotions...")? These assumptions might be fine if your children perfectly fit the stereotype for their gender but can lead to problems if your children defy any of the expectations. Your son's aggression may be ignored at school (because boys, after all, will be boys), but your daughter may be punished for the same behavior. One behavior, such as play fighting, can be labeled rambunctious for boys and aggressive for girls. It's all because of the lens we are using. When seen through the lens of gender, "atypical" behavior may be seen as a problem when really it is simply not fitting a stereotype.

## Math Abilities

We all know about the very famous gender difference in math abilities, right? Every few years there is a news story that agitates everyone about girls' innate abilities in math. Barbie uttered the phrase, "Math class is tough" and was quickly reprogrammed. Larry Summers, the former president of Harvard, resigned not long after suggesting in a 2005 speech that there were innate differences in mathematical abilities that kept women from becoming science and engineering professors.

It seems like everyone, to a degree, believes in this gender difference. Many parents believe it. In one study, fathers, on average, estimated their sons' mathematical IQ at 110 and their daughters' at 98. Moms are not exempt either. In the same study, mothers, on average, estimated their sons' mathematical IQ to be 110 and their daughters' to be 104.[11] Many teachers also believe it. Studies have repeatedly shown that they rate boys' math ability higher than girls'.[12] Even kids believe it. When asked how good they believe they are at math, elementary school boys often report feeling significantly stronger at math than do girls.[13]

If so many people believe that boys are better at math than girls are, then surely that must be accurate... Well, not really—it is much more complicated than that. In a meta-analysis conducted in 1990, results indicated that girls were better at simple computation in elementary and middle school, and boys were better at complex problem-solving in high school.[14] But a more recent study, conducted in 2008, found that those gender differences no longer exist. In an analysis of statewide math standardized tests given from 2005 to 2007, there were no gender differences at all in mathematics performance.[15]

There are some gender differences related to math, however. Ironically, counter to the stereotype, girls actually earn higher grades in math classes than boys through high school. Even more ironically, given that girls are earning higher grades, the biggest gender difference relates to how boys and girls feel about their math abilities. Girls feel more anxious about math and less self-confident about their abilities than boys. Boys are also more motivated to do well in math than girls (although no one knows exactly why). So, despite no differences on standardized math tests and better performance in math class, girls feel less capable and more anxious about math than boys.[16] It's a head-scratcher.

This paradox is not hard to find in real life. I once led a discussion group with high-achieving undergraduates, all women, while I was a professor at UCLA. I made the point that many, many women assume they are bad at math, but those women also assume it is an insecurity specific to them and not based on their gender. When I asked them to raise their hands if they felt insecure about their math abilities, they all raised their hands, shocked that the entire group felt the same way. Feeling bold, I told them I would wager a bet that if I asked a similar group of men, almost no one would raise their hand. We ventured down the hall, found a group of men in a classroom, and asked the same question. As I predicted, no man raised his hand. Who knows how good or bad at math anyone actually was, but there was an obvious difference in math self-confidence between the men and women.

## Reflection

Stereotypes about gender have affected you, just as much as they affect your kids. Think for a second about yourself. Are you good at math? If you are a woman, I would bet money—if I knew you and could actually collect—that you say either (1) you are not very good at math or (2) you do not like math. If you are a man—congratulations for reading a parenting book; you have upended that stereotype about women being the most concerned parent. But how often do you talk to someone about your feelings, particularly if something makes you sad? The answer is probably "very rarely."

These differences are not innate. They are not based on abilities in math or in expressing sadness. They are the result of cultural stereotypes that tagged you while you weren't looking.

## Verbal Abilities

There is a strong and pervasive stereotype that women are more talkative than men. Recently, after discussing over dinner how Grace could talk to herself for hours, a close family friend said, "Well, you know about the research showing that women are twice as talkative as men." He was very specific, but totally inaccurate.

Professor Campbell Leaper, an expert on gender differences in childhood and adolescence at the University of California, Santa Cruz, conducted a different meta-analysis, this one on forty-six different studies of talkativeness. According to him, the gender difference in talkativeness is "negligible." In fact, the only gender difference was among one- to three-year-old kids. Among children between ages three and thirteen (the oldest group included in the study), no gender differences existed at all. Even among the toddlers, there was only a difference if the study was done in a lab setting; there were no gender differences if the study was conducted at home or school.[17]

There are some slight differences in what type of language boys and girls use, however. Girls are slightly more likely than boys to use what is referred to as affiliative speech (e.g., to offer praise, agree with the person they are talking to, or elaborate on the other person's comments). Boys, on the other hand, are slightly more likely than girls to use assertive speech (e.g., to give information or make a suggestion, disagree with the other person, criticize, or offer an opinion). In other words, boys and girls don't really differ in how much they talk, just what they use those words for.

Although kids don't really differ in talkativeness, there are some small differences in how kids develop their verbal skills. Girls tend to develop language earlier than boys, and girls on average tend to score higher than boys on verbal production (that is, the number of words they can say). So your three-year-old daughter might use more words than your three-year-old nephew. This can be reassuring to the parent of a son who is obsessing about why his son says fewer words than his friend's daughter. This doesn't translate into long term differences, though, as there are no differences in vocabulary or reading comprehension by school age.

There is a small danger in knowing that there is a gender difference in verbal production at early ages. Early in my career, I helped manage a research project that followed children with autism from toddlerhood on to figure out what interventions (such as speech or occupational therapy) were most helpful as they developed. After that experience, I have always had my radar out for autism.

Some years ago, I had a friend whose son had said only a couple of words by the time he was three years old. He would grunt from time to time, point at crackers when he wanted crackers, and point at milk when he wanted milk, but he wasn't really babbling or talking. I had seen enough three-year-olds with autism to recognize it pretty quickly, so I was concerned about this boy's clearly delayed speech at age three as that can be an important sign of autism. My friend, however, was convinced her son was slow to speak simply because he was a boy. She overlooked many warning signs (he was also less affectionate than most small children) because she stubbornly held on to her belief in a big gender difference. Finally, a pediatrician convinced her that he was delayed, even compared to other boys. This is an extreme example, but it was heartbreaking to watch misinformation on gender differences in language prevent a mother from catching some warning signs. The difference between when boys and girls develop language is not years; it is, at most, the difference of a couple of months.

## Self-Esteem, Depression, and Body Image

A prevailing assumption also persists that girls generally feel worse about themselves than boys. There is some truth to this assumption, although it is not quite that straightforward. Do girls have worse self-esteem than boys? Do they feel less positive about their unique qualities? Sometimes the answer is yes. But, according to meta-analyses, the gender differences are small when the studies examine white kids. And if the studies focus on African-American children, the gender difference is nonexistent—overall, boys and girls feel equally positive or negative about themselves.[18]

However, there is a big difference in how boys and girls feel about their bodies. Even when their bodies are within a normal body-weight range, girls are more likely to be unhappy with their weight than boys. More than 70 percent of girls between the ages of twelve and eighteen are unhappy with their bodies, compared to only 40 percent of boys. This body dissatisfaction starts as early at third grade.[19] Unhappiness with body image is closely tied to media consumption. The more television that children and adolescents watch, the more unhappy they are with their bodies. Body dissatisfaction is also closely linked with girls developing depression.[20] A strong emphasis on being attractive and thin is hard to live up to, especially as girls enter the zit-producing, hip-enlarging phase of puberty. Falling short of that ideal is linked with feeling bad about oneself. Boys are considerably more immune from these attractiveness pressures.[21]

What about at the far end of the spectrum—depression—where feelings about oneself are most negative? Contrary to what most people assume, before adolescence kicks in, boys are actually at a slightly greater risk of suffering from depression than girls.[22] In the middle of puberty, however, there is a sharp increase in the number of girls who are diagnosed with depression. By adolescence, girls are twice as likely as boys to suffer from depression. This gender difference sticks around for the rest of adulthood. Explanations for it are varied, and include biological, cognitive, and social theories. Oftentimes, people search for biological causes, because the gender difference shifts at about the time of puberty. But there is not a great deal of support for this explanation.[23] It is likely that biological factors play some role, although it is still unclear exactly what that role is.

Two researchers, Benjamin Hankin from the University of Illinois at Chicago and Lyn Abramson from the University of Wisconsin-Madison, reviewed massive amounts of research on depression and suggest an explanation for why, with the onset of puberty, girls are more likely to become depressed than boys.[24] Much of their explanation for the gender difference in depression has to do with how boys and girls deal with stressful events. When negative events happen to girls, they are more likely than boys to play the event over and over again in their minds. This process, called rumination, is like programming the CD player to replay the same set of songs again and again. When the event that gets replayed is negative, girls, who are more likely than boys to ruminate, become increasingly distressed.

According to Hankin and Abramson, this effect is compounded because girls also are more likely than boys to be aware of negative life events, such as conflict among peers or parents. So girls notice negative events and replay them repeatedly. And because they are socialized to be allowed to talk about their feelings of sadness—which can lead to even more rumination over past sad events—girls are more likely to end up depressed. Boys, however, are less likely than girls to notice the negative exchanges that take place around them, and when they do notice them, they are less likely to ruminate on them.[25] Plus they are socialized to express not sadness but anger and frustration. While expressing anger and frustration can be problematic, it's a good way to avoid depression. Which leads us to...

## Aggression

If you had spent all of your life in a cave and recently emerged and stumbled into a Toys "R" Us, you would (after recovering from the total sensory overload) learn two things about children: girls like dolls, and boys are aggressive. Most of the toys in the boys' aisle involve some type of violence: guns, action figures with guns, video games with guns, ball throwers shaped like guns, and so on. And this observation is backed up pretty well by research.

In Hyde's meta-analysis of forty-six meta-analyses, one of the biggest gender differences to emerge was not the overall rates of aggression, but specific types of aggression.[26] When a child is provoked, he or she is likely to be physically aggressive at basically the same rates for boys and girls. But in incidences of unprovoked physical aggression, boys physically lash out significantly more than girls. This is partially why men are much more likely to commit a violent crime than women (for example, men are seven times more likely to commit murder than women).[27]

What about the stereotype that girls are more verbally and relationally aggressive? Think about the movie *Mean Girls*, in which a popular group of girls wield power by spreading rumors, criticizing, and selectively excluding some girls from their group; this definitely happens in real life. My sister-in-law told me a story about a trend among the girls at my niece's elementary school. Some girls like to taunt others by saying, "You are my best friend now, but she will be my best friend forever." Ouch! But despite the persistence of this stereotype (even in my own thinking), there is no difference in the amount of social aggression displayed by boys and girls. At best, girls may be more sophisticated (or cleverly mean) than boys in their use of this type of social aggression.[28]

## Play and Sports

Next time you visit your child's school, take a detour by the playground. If kids are at recess, you are likely to witness the single biggest gender difference there is—play styles. Most often, boys are playing in a large group, frequently in a pseudo-organized game of some kind such as kickball, basketball, dodgeball, or soccer. The choice of game is determined by what equipment is available and how the playground is configured. But the style of play is consistent: boys tend to play some kind of high-intensity, active, team-based game with two teams and a score. Someone often ends up hurt: skinned knees and bruised shins seem to be part of the initiation into boyhood.

Now look at the periphery of the playground: girls are often on the swings and monkey bars or playing four-square, jump rope, or hopscotch. They aren't divided into large teams, and they aren't keeping score. They are likely to be playing one on one. They may be playing the same hand-slap singsong games I did as a child. I was surprised one day when Maya came home singing, "Cinderella, dressed in yellow, went upstairs to kiss her fella. Made a mistake, kissed a snake. How many doctors did it take?" My husband had never heard this song before, but I could recite it in my sleep. It was a holdover of my own elementary school days where we would sing this while jump-roping to see how high we could count before tripping. The boys never participated; their kickball game kept them busy. Indeed, the playground hasn't changed much. Clothes may be different, and the popular phrases may have changed (my own '80s Valley Girl "Gag me with a spoon" has been replaced by "OMG"), but the types of games and the boys-over-here and girls-over-there landscape looks the same.

This play segregation by gender begins in preschool, around age three. Esteemed developmental psychologist Eleanor Maccoby, a long-time Stanford professor, carefully documented this segregation in pre-school play. She argues that there are small differences in activity level in early childhood that lead slightly quieter girls to gravitate toward other quiet girls, and slightly more active boys to gravitate toward other active boys.[29] These small clusters of similar girls and similar boys ultimately grow into more widespread segregated play. As Maccoby describes it, during preschool, children learn that gender is a "social category." Girls want to play only with girls and boys only with boys, so even the more active girls choose to play with other girls because they belong to the "right" category, and the quieter boys choose other boys just because they are boys. Over time, more and more girls play quietly on one side of the playground and more and more boys play physically on the other side.

Kids begin to socialize themselves in the ways of their gender by playing exclusively with other kids of the same gender. In this way, girls and boys learn the unwritten rules of being in their gender group. Maccoby states that, by socializing each other, girls become more girlish and boys become more boyish, and it gets harder and harder to meet in the middle and play together. These small biological differences in activity levels lead to grouping by gender, and the grouping leads to shaping each others' play styles, which only leads to bigger differences later in childhood. The end result is an elementary school playground that looks like Moses came by and parted it.

# SITUATION MATTERS

As humans, we like to think we are who we are, regardless of the situation. Ha! Much of the field of social psychology exists because a situation can sometimes be more powerful than any individual. Some situations bring out gender differences that wouldn't exist otherwise. Smiling is an example: A meta-analysis examined how much people smile. The results show that there are no gender differences in smiling in children. Boys and girls, delightfully, smile often and the same amount. Once they hit the teenage years, a gender difference emerges. As you might guess, women on average smile more often than men. But—and this is a big but—that difference is much more pronounced if the women knew they were being watched. Women don't differ much from men when they are oblivious to having an audience.[30]

A similar phenomenon occurs with helping others. When it seems that no one is watching, men and women are just as likely to help a stranger. When there is an audience, however, men helped considerably more often than women did.[31] These studies tell us that there is something about the different social roles we play that leads to some of the differences we see. And we seem to step into our social roles, roles in which women are friendly and men are helpers, when called into public action. In some ways, we are like actors on a stage, each playing out a stereotyped script.

# EXPERIENCE MATTERS

David Tzuriel and Gila Egozi, researchers at the School of Education at Bar Ilan University in Israel, aren't gender researchers. They study children's cognitive abilities and whether training can shape those abilities. They recently made a very significant discovery about the importance of boys' and girls' experiences in developing their cognitive skills. They were interested in testing the assumption that boys were biologically better than girls at spatial abilities,[32] largely the ability to mentally rotate shapes and see shapes from multiple perspectives. Spatial ability is one math-based skill that does show a gender difference, and it's the only math-based skill not taught in schools. Some evolutionary psychologists have argued that this difference, in which boys are better able to mentally represent shapes than girls, is a holdover from our evolutionary past where men had to leave the home to hunt and needed to know how to get back to the hut without getting lost.

The researchers suspected, however, that boys and girls might have vastly different experiences with spatial tasks and wondered how dependent these abilities were on those experiences. They taught first-grade boys and girls to visualize shapes in multiple ways. For example, the kids thought about the object below as a hexagon with an X, bow ties, two kites, diamonds, and an open envelope.

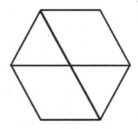

Guess what? After several of these training sessions, the gender gap in spatial abilities completely disappeared. The researchers concluded that girls simply have less experience with spatial tasks than boys. Given the same amount of practice that boys have in their regular lives (think hours of playing blocks and Legos), girls can do just as well. Other studies have supported the conclusion that if girls get practice, the difference disappears. When girls play video games as much as boys, their ability to mentally rotate objects also improves.[33] So much for that biological difference.

# THE FINAL FOUR:
# WHAT ARE THE KEY ISSUES?

- When thinking about gender differences, pay attention to whether the research focuses on babies, children, or adults. Knowing that adults differ along gendered lines tells us little about innate, inevitable differences.

- By looking at all the research on gender differences, we see there are very few actual differences between boys and girls. The hundreds of studies that find zero differences are published less often, and are also less likely to be splashed on the cover of *Time*.

- The only real differences between boys and girls are in the ability to control their impulses, in their interest and self-confidence in math, in the timing of their first words, in their body image and post-puberty depression, in their unprovoked aggression, and in their play styles.

- Many of the differences we do see become more pronounced with age, or are observed in children who were never taught how to use a specific skill. Other differences are most obvious when they help people fit into their social role (such as "smiling woman" or "man to the rescue").

## CHAPTER 5

# How Different Is Different?

**News stories are quick to point out** studies showing gender differences. In November 2012, a study was presented at Radiological Society of North America about the progression of Alzheimer's disease in men and women. A press release quickly followed.[1] Many news reports and websites jumped on the finding and reported that "In men, the disease developed more aggressively in a shorter period of time."[2] This is interesting, but there are important follow-up questions that never get answered in the sound bite or headline. How much more aggressively and in what time frame does the disease progress for men? Do women have ten years and men only one year from diagnosis to full-blown cognitive impairment, or do women have ten years and men have nine years? These are very different scenarios, all falling under the umbrella of a gender difference. Also, is the progression of Alzheimer's ever more aggressive in women than men? Books titled *Boys and Girls Learn Differently!* rarely give these kinds of details about the differences. Nuance doesn't usually sell books or make a good sound bite or Tweet. To understand what a gender difference really means, we need to know how different "different" is.

When you hear on the evening news that a recent study found a gender difference in Alzheimer's progression, aggression, school performance, or brain development, know that what the researchers really found was a statistical difference. Researchers collected scores from boys and girls and then averaged all the boys' scores and all the girls' scores. Being statistically different means that the researchers are 95 percent certain that the differences between the two groups are not a random fluke. It actually has little to do with how different that difference is and more about the probability of boys and girls being consistently different. Also, the more children included in the study, the smaller that statistical difference needs to be. So if I tested the IQ of one thousand boys and one thousand girls, and girls scored 100.15 and boys scored 99.85, that would qualify as statistically different. I can say that based on the statistical analyses I used, I am 95 percent certain that the two groups do indeed differ. Should I claim on the news that girls are smarter than boys? Probably not. Could I even perceive the difference between children with IQs of 100.15 and 99.85? Probably not.

## Reflection

We often overlook the variability between kids of the same gender. Think about your child and his or her best friend. Think of the five biggest ways in which they differ from one another. It is pretty easy, isn't it? Keep in mind, these are kids who are the same gender, same age, likely the same socioeconomic background, usually attend the same school, and are similar enough to become best friends. Yet, even with all those similarities, the individuals shine through.

## KNOW THE VARIATION

Jacob Cohen, a statistician, created a pretty simple formula to help determine how different a difference is. The answer to the formula, which is called an effect size, compares the differences between groups

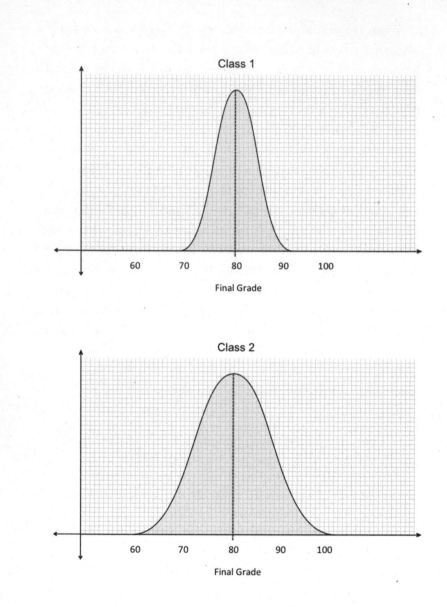

Different distributions of grades from two different hypothetical classes with the same average grade.

to the differences between members of the same group. It tells us, for example, whether boys differ from girls more than from other boys. More often, it tells us that the differences between girls and those between boys are greater than the group differences between the average boy and girl. If I had two classrooms, one of all girls and one of all boys, I might want to know whether the variation within each class is bigger than the differences between the two classes. Effect size is the answer to that question.

The first key to determining the size of the effect is to know how much boys and girls vary in their traits, skills, and behaviors. Some traits and behaviors are simply more variable than others. Look at the two graphs on page 74. Both represent the final grades from two different college classes. As a student, you need to enroll in one class, obviously wanting the one in which you are most likely to get an A.

In both classes, the average grade is an 80, a B. In Class 1, you can see that there is not much variation around that 80. No student was more than 10 points above or below the average. In other words, no students failed, but no students received an A either. In Class 2, the variation is much bigger, 20 points. Some students had a 60, a disappointing D, but others maxed out with a perfect grade. If you want an A, you are going to take the second class. The risk for doing poorly is higher, but so is the potential payoff of doing well.

The issue of variability also matters when thinking about the differences between boys and girls. For every trait, skill, preference, or behavior ever measured, there is a distribution like the ones mentioned above. Boys and girls each have a distribution, which almost always looks like these bell curves: most people fall near the average, and fewer and fewer people fall at either end of the spectrum.

Steve Strand and colleagues at the University of Warwick in the United Kingdom noticed that there were a lot of media reports about boys falling behind girls in school and boys being academically "in crisis." Indeed, in 2002 in the United Kingdom, 57 percent of girls were passing all of their school subjects compared to 46 percent of boys. This wasn't seen in English classes only; these were also the results in "boy subjects" like math, business, science, and computers. The researchers investigated the childrens' IQ tests and scores from the Cognitive Abilities Test and found that boys and girls performed similarly.[3]

However, boys' scores were more variable: when asked to solve algebra-like problems, for example, boys' scores were 18 percent more variable than girls' scores. Even though their average scores were similar, boys were more likely to be among the top performers and among the bottom performers, compared to girls. In this case, it's misleading to state that boys are stronger than girls at algebra; it glosses over a larger-than-expected number of low-performing boys, leaving them to struggle at the bottom of the scale.

To really compare boys and girls, we have to lay these distributions on top of one another and see how much they overlap. The graph below shows the actual overlapping distribution between the self-esteem of men and women. As you can see, the average scores differ, but they share a lot of common ground. In fact, if I was asked to randomly pick out a kid with low self-esteem, I am just as likely to pick a boy as a girl.

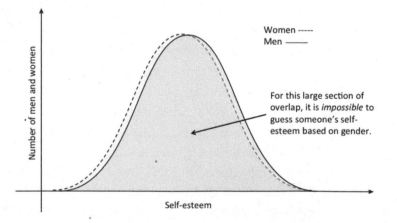

This shows the approximate difference between the self-esteem of men and women. The effect size is 0.20. More than three-quarters of all gender differences are smaller than this.

# WHAT'S THE EFFECT SIZE?

Researchers have calculated effect sizes for all the gender differences discussed in the previous chapter. Meta-analyses report these, comparing how different boys and girls as a group are compared to individual boys and individual girls.

Think back to Janet Hyde's massive meta-meta-analysis of 124 different gender differences across more than one million people.[4] Of those 124 differences, she found that 30 percent of the findings had an effect size near 0. An effect size near 0 means that, if I presented you with two students—a girl and a boy—and asked you to pick the best math student, you would only have a 50-50 chance of being right. You might as well flip a coin. Knowing the gender of the child provides no extra information. The distributions overlap perfectly.

There were some differences, of course. But how big were those differences? Of the 124 gender differences, 48 percent were considered very small, with effect sizes between 0.11 and 0.20. The graph showing boys' and girls' self-esteem illustrates an effect size of 0.20, one of the bigger effect sizes Hyde found. If I presented you with the same boy and girl described earlier and asked you to pick the one with the best self-esteem, you would have a 54 percent chance of being right by picking the boy. Jacob Cohen said differences of this size are not really noticeable in real life.[5] According to Cohen, one way to visualize a difference this small is to think about comparing the height of a fifteen- and a sixteen-year-old girl.

Taken together, this means that 78 percent of all the gender differences included in the meta-analysis of more than a million people found gender differences so small that, if all I knew about a kid was his or her gender, I would only have—at most—a 54 percent chance of picking the kid who exhibits more of a specific difference. In other words, it's not much better than chance. Remember, these were areas that were supposed to be different, like math skills, verbal abilities, and emotional expression. Yet, for more than three-quarters of all these supposed gender differences, gender only tells us a little more about a person than we would know by flipping a coin. Knowing the gender of a person doesn't reveal who is better at math, reading, showing sadness, or being scared.

Some of the differences were a little bigger. Indeed, 15 percent of the differences were considered "medium." If I asked you to pick the boy or girl who was most likely to be physically aggressive, you would have a 60 percent chance of guessing right if you picked the boy. As Cohen said, these differences are noticeable but not overwhelmingly obvious, like the difference between the heights of a fourteen- and an eighteen-year-old girl.

The only "large" differences are in how fast and far a child can throw a ball and in some sexual behaviors (such as the frequency of reported masturbation). So, for my money, gender is only really helpful if I am picking out a baseball player or deciding who most needs to chat about appropriate times and places to masturbate. Otherwise, the odds of being right aren't overwhelming.

There are several ways to conceptualize effect sizes in real life. Take two examples of ways that boys and girls are assumed to be very different: activity level and verbal skills.

Boys are considered to be much more active than girls. In infancy, the gender difference has an effect size of 0.21.[6] What does that mean in real life? Assume Jason is an average infant boy with an average activity level for a boy his age. He wiggles around when his mom tries to unload groceries, flaps his arms when he sees the dog, grabs at the car keys and cell phone, and constantly tries to pull himself up on the couch's edge. Jason is simply average, with half of the other boys being more active than him and half being less active.

What about girls? Because boys' and girls' distributions for activity level overlap so much, 42 percent of girls are actually more active than Jason. So we can't really say that girls are less active than boys. We can say that 58 percent of girls are less active than the average boy, but then again, so are 50 percent of boys.

There is yet another way to conceptualize effect sizes. It is commonly reported that girls have stronger verbal abilities than boys. Girls say words earlier, develop more words more quickly, speak in longer sentences, have larger vocabularies, and understand what they read better. The effect size for these verbal skills is 0.11.[7] How does this translate into real life? Imagine I go to Maya's elementary school and give all of the third graders a test of verbal skills. There are, conveniently, twenty-five boys and twenty-five girls. I then have the children form two lines—a girls' line and a boys' line, each ordered from best score to worst. Maggie scores exactly in the midpoint of all the girls: twelve girls stand ahead of her and twelve stand behind. Maggie gets the exact same score on her verbal test as Michael. But there are fewer boys than girls who score as high as Maggie. How many? How big is the effect? Maggie bests twelve of the girls with her verbal skills and bests thirteen of the boys. That's a difference, no doubt, but I would refuse to tailor my classroom or parenting style on that small a difference.

Every time you hear about gender differences, keep in mind how different they really are. Is it only the difference between ranking twelfth or thirteenth? If so, you have to decide for yourself whether that is meaningful. For the vast majority of all the gender differences included in the big Hyde study (78 percent of them), this is as large as the difference gets.

## IT'S ALL IN THE COMPARISON

If boys as a group aren't really very different from girls as a group, and knowing a person's gender doesn't help us much in predicting anything about an individual (except for what color he or she is wearing and what toys are in the toy box), does that mean gender doesn't matter?

It does matter, and it's particularly important if you have a son and a daughter. Parents notice the subtle differences between their kids no matter who the children are. I frequently compare my own two girls: Grace throws more tantrums than Maya ever did, but Grace could climb the jungle gym at age two while Maya didn't until age five. We constantly make these comparisons, even when we have the sense to keep it to ourselves. It is hard not to compare. I thought I had kids figured out with Maya, and then Grace comes along and does everything differently. It wasn't that my excellent parenting skills taught Maya to be compliant. I do the same things with Grace that I did with Maya, with much different effects. Grace taught me that Maya was just born compliant. So I have to rethink my expectations.

But when we have a son and a daughter, those subtle differences are often linked to gender. If Grace had been a boy, my stereotypes about boys being more active, aggressive, and athletic would have been confirmed. Even though the differences between kids are just the natural differences between individuals, when they fall along gender lines, we tend to exaggerate the differences.

Imagine you have fraternal twins, Jack and Jill. Jill has slightly better verbal abilities than Jack. She can say 450 words and Jack says 400. If they were the same gender, you wouldn't notice the slight difference. You would assume that this is the normal variability that comes along with individuals. If Jack had more words, you wouldn't think much of it. We tend to overlook and ignore the instances that don't support our stereotypes (as described in chapter 3), so this would probably get glossed over. But because the difference corresponds with the stereotype that girls are more verbal than boys, we are likely to attribute the difference to gender ("Just like you'd expect, our girl is the real talker in the family"). We do this, even though the difference is very small.

Among siblings, these comparisons are critical. If you have a sibling, do you remember how you all developed his or her "role" in the family. One child becomes the reader, one the math whiz, one the comedian, one the athlete. One child is the sensitive one and one, the hothead. Even though, by any objective measure, siblings are largely similar, the small differences are exaggerated within the family. When those differences fit the stereotypes (and they usually have a 50-50 chance of fitting the stereotype), those small differences get noticed and reinforced.

Ann Crouter and Susan McHale, developmental psychologists at Pennsylvania State University, are experts on how the gender composition of families impacts each child's development. They find that families with a son and daughter often exaggerate the gender differences in their family. For example, parents assign more stereotypical chores to their kids when they have both a boy and a girl. The boy mows the lawn and takes out the trash, and the girl empties the dishwasher and helps clean the house.[8]

Differences also get exaggerated because parents are more likely to pair off with their same-gender child. Mom will take daughter to the mall, and Dad will take son to the basketball game. The daughter, then, is less likely to watch basketball games and less likely to learn how to mow the lawn. Perhaps she would have been the child more interested in sports, but simply because she was born with a brother, her natural place in the distribution was overlooked.

## Reflection

If you have children of different genders, notice the times your children approach a situation differently, perhaps on the first day of a new school or summer camp. Think about how they react to a sad or a frightening situation. Also notice the times they react similarly. Do the same if you have children of the same gender—notice the times they react differently and similarly. Our human nature leads us to exaggerate both the differences between groups and the similarities within groups, so we have to pay attention to all the times those rules don't apply.

## KNOWING GENDER ISN'T EVERYTHING

I am guessing that most people don't care much about statistics or how to calculate an effect size (most of my graduate students in statistics classes don't care much about statistics either!). But understanding effect sizes is important; it helps us better raise our children (something we care a great deal about). Effect sizes matter because they show us that most of the things we think are due to gender are frequently random. Given such small effect sizes, knowing someone's gender means we have about a 50-50 chance of being right when it comes to predicting their personality traits, skills, and abilities (with a 60-40 chance at best). If I am trying to decide which summer camp to enroll my child in, which classes to sign her up for, which learning strategy to use, or which behaviors to encourage, knowing what the "typical" girl or boy is like tells me very little about my individual child; there is simply too much variability and overlap between girls and boys.

So I have two options: I can choose activities completely at random with a flip of a coin. Or better, and what I actually suggest, I can focus on the individual child and consider her gender to be just as informative and important as her height, strength, hair color, and all of her other biological characteristics—just as informative, but not more important.

The process of paying less attention to gender and more to the individual child begins by noticing how little gender really predicts our own children's skills and abilities. Because we tend to exaggerate the differences between groups but overlook the differences within them, we rely on stereotypes without intending to. The goal, then, is to start paying more attention to each individual child.

I have been blessed by having two daughters. It makes seeing differences within the same gender pretty easy because their differences are so clear. Sometimes one child fits the stereotype for girls, and sometimes she doesn't. One child isn't more stereotypical than the other; it simply depends on the issue. To return to the previous example, Grace is much more athletic than Maya: She climbs playground equipment meant for much older children, often in pursuit of her older sister. And even though she is young, she is much more aware of her body's movement and position than is Maya (who could be compared to a bull shopping for china). So we don't push sports for Maya. She plays them, but the goal is always to have fun, not to keep score. In fact, sports scores are rarely discussed in our family. Maya plays the piano and violin and shines beautifully. Grace is goal-oriented, strong, and eager to throw a ball; sports call her name.

Maya is also much more sensitive than Grace. From birth, she was attuned to other people and their feelings. She continues to be sensitive—upset if she feels she has disappointed you, quick to help friends settle disputes, and putting others' feelings above her own. Grace really couldn't care less how you feel. She has focus and purpose, and your feelings may be mere obstacles in her way. For Grace, I try to teach empathy and attending to others' feelings. I point it out in stories, "Look. She seems frustrated, doesn't she?" Grace doesn't cry from sadness but from frustration, not like the stereotype, and not like her sister.

Yet Grace is no "tomboy." She likes to be clean, gets stressed when something gets on her clothes, is most content in her Minnie Mouse shoes, usually wants a barrette, and always has an opinion about her outfit. On this front, Maya couldn't care less. She loves a particular pair of socks that she wears with everything, regardless of whether they match. She wears whatever random outfit I lay out for her, as long as it is comfortable, and she never notices the black line of dirt under her nails. Grace is extremely verbal, speaking in complex sentences far beyond her years. Maya is very gifted in math.

They each have moments when, if I had to pick them out of a distribution of girls, they would be on the stereotypical "girly" end of the spectrum. But that's only on certain issues, and not on the same issues for both of them. Maya cries easily, and Grace talks all the time. They also have moments where, because boys' and girls' distributions overlap so much, they would be on the stereotypical "boyish" end of the bell curve. Maya is a math whiz and Grace is very strong. The unique combinations of traits and abilities fall within normal ranges for girls. If I had two boys, I could describe them with the exact same words, and the mix would still be perfectly normal for boys as well.

# FEWER CATEGORIES, MORE CONTINUUMS

Boys and girls are not two distinct, nonoverlapping categories. Even though it is easier to think that each group has a set of core characteristics, it doesn't work like that. There is too much variation within each group, and more importantly, too much variation within each individual child.

In individual kids (and adults), every trait, skill, ability, or behavior falls on its own distribution or continuum. Sometimes, compared to the average girl or boy, your child is above the gender average for one trait (like Maya at math and Grace in strength) and below the gender average for another trait (like Maya with her lack of appearance concerns and Grace in empathy). And sometimes they fit the stereotype completely (like Maya in her pink room and Grace with her Minnie Mouse shoes). It just depends on the trait, skill, or behavior. All are perfectly normal. Sometimes your son will be very verbal, terrible at math and sports, and very sensitive. This isn't weird or atypical; it makes him a perfectly normal boy. Children fall on continuums, not into categories.

Similarly, the term "tomboy" drives me nuts. It presumes that being athletic or active or better at tree climbing than nail painting is not the norm for a girl and requires a special label. Women often describe themselves as tomboys as children. Pop star Britney Spears recently told a newspaper she is a tomboy because she doesn't leave the house in full makeup every day. Perhaps, instead of labeling an athletic girl or one who doesn't live for makeup, we could just recognize that not all girls are alike. The variation is the norm.

# THE FINAL FOUR:
## WHAT ARE THE KEY ISSUES?

- For most traits and abilities, boys differ from other boys and girls differ from other girls more than the two groups differ from each other. Just because we like to ignore the variation within a group of boys or a group of girls doesn't mean it doesn't exist.

- Even when the average boy differs from the average girl, the distributions are often largely overlapping. This means we cannot really predict what a child will be like based on his or her gender.

- We sometimes assume that random differences between individuals are due to gender. This is especially difficult to avoid when we have a son and a daughter. Pay attention to the chores you assign each child and which parent pairs off with each child.

- Try to notice the times your same-gender children differ from one another and your different-gender children are similar. These instances happen all the time, but you might be overlooking them.

# Decoding Neuroscience

**The brain is largely a mystery.** Humans are drawn to the mystery and think that once we understand the brain, we will understand all human behavior. Yet, despite enormous advances in neuroscience, scientists are still grappling with the ways that an extremely complex brain drives extremely complex behaviors. Unfortunately, the complicated issues involved in neuroscience are rarely conveyed in the sound-bite news coverage of research on the brain.

Most of you have likely heard about how boys and girls learn differently because of differences in their brains. These claims are typically conveyed in a news story in which we are shown an image of a brain, with brightly glowing regions in red and yellow, and told a broad claim about behavior (such as "Boys only use one part of their brain at a time!"). These studies get so much coverage, in part, because they seem so straightforward and intuitively make sense. We see different regions of the brain "glowing" differently, and we know that men and women behave differently. Therefore, the brain differences must be causing the behavior differences in boys and girls. We put a lot of weight on those glowing images of the brain.

The claims about differences in the brain causing the behavioral differences between boys and girls are also a pretty lucrative business, a business that is influencing how our children are being educated. Authors Michael Gurian and Leonard Sax have made lots of money selling the idea of "brain-based" gender differences to school districts around the country. For a fee, your child's teacher can attend the Gurian Institute in Colorado and learn about the myriad ways that boys' and girls' brains differ. Teachers come back to their own schools after lessons at the institute, armed with PowerPoint slides of brain scans. More glowing images of brains. Based on these supposed brain-based differences, they recommend entirely different educational curricula for boys and girls (discussed in detail in chapter 11).

The problem with blindly trusting these broad claims about behavior, simply because they are associated with images of the brain, is that many of the claims are false, and not just a little false either. For example, the findings discussed in *The Female Brain* by Louann Brizendine[1] are so false that the journal *Nature* described it as "riddled with scientific errors."[2] But we will come back to all of the false claims in a minute.

In this chapter, I describe what some authors claim to be the differences in the brains of boys and girls and how it's harmful:

- I explain how they are using those claims to manipulate your child's education.

- I steal from the work of neuroscientists who have detailed the many flaws in those claims.

- I point out what the actual, reliable differences are between boys' and girls' brains.

My job here isn't to go into extensive detail about the neuroscience of gender. If you are interested in reading further, I recommend *Delusions of Gender* by Cordelia Fine; *Pink Brain, Blue Brain* by Lise Eliot; and *Brain Storm: The Flaws in the Science of Sex Differences* by Rebecca Jordan-Young. My goal is to boil down others' work to the most basic findings, to point out what is myth and what is real, and most importantly, to help you use this information in your own life.

Even if you don't read a book about neuroscience, the findings may have an impact on you. Your children's brains drive their thoughts, motivations, and feelings. The experiences they have, from the womb to the first day home to every day after, shape their brains in permanent ways. Experiences are more important, and more permanent, than you may think. And you are shaping your baby's brain—the structure, function, and organization—from the day you become pregnant. No pressure or anything!

## HISTORY REPEATS ITSELF

We have a long history of looking to the brain to explain differences between men and women. About 150 years ago, scientists studying the brain (most of whom were male) thought that the size of the brain determined intelligence. They would fill empty skulls with seeds and then dump out and weigh the seeds, figuring that the more seeds there are, the larger the skull; the larger the skull, the larger the brain; the larger the brain, the smarter the person. This logic fit their worldview of men as more innately intelligent than women. Someone then raised a troubling question. If larger brains meant greater intelligence, then how do we explain elephants? Since no one was concerned that elephants were going to start enrolling in college, scientists of the time had to revise their working theory. The revision is a classic example of the tail wagging the dog. They assumed at the time that women had smaller frontal lobes and larger parietal lobes than men. Therefore, because women were clearly inferior, frontal lobes must be the source of intelligence. But by the turn of the century, scientific thinking sourced the seat of intelligence to the parietal lobe. So new scientists "discovered" that women, in fact, did not have larger parietal lobes after all. In other words, the source of intelligence was whatever women had less of than men.

Our techniques have improved greatly since 1900. We now have sophisticated machines that scan for the amount of blood flow that goes to certain cells in the brain while the individual is talking, looking at certain images, or thinking certain thoughts. Now, these functional MRIs are the norm in neuroscience research, replacing seeds in a skull as the measurement of choice. For example, researchers slide a man or a woman into the long tube of the machine and ask the research participant to look at fearful faces and think about what the person in the picture is thinking. The fMRI measures the blood flow in each person's brain while they are thinking about the fearful face. The researcher then compares the two scans to see if there are any differences in blood flow between the man and the woman (many studies only scan eight men and eight women, average each gender group's scans together, and then compare men's average to women's average). Blood flow is a proxy for brain activity. If there is a difference, the researcher claims that men and women process emotion differently. So the pretty brain scans you see glowing yellow and red indicate where the differences are; they do not indicate where the brain "lights up." In fact, oftentimes, the tail is still wagging the dog. As you will see, although we have improved from the days of simply looking at skull size, there is still a lot of room for improvement when it comes to understanding the brain.

## BRAIN BIO 101

Most everyone agrees on the basics about the brain in general, and about boys and girls specifically; you might have picked up some of this in a biology class in high school. In the spirit of this book, I discuss how we are the same before describing how we are different. Keep in mind that while I am usually describing what happens when everything goes right in brain development, with so much complexity and so many possible glitches, everything going right isn't something to take for granted.

## What Are the Similarities?

What is the same for everyone? At birth, we possess about one hundred billion nerve cells, or neurons, a mind-boggling number, and will have basically the same number of neurons throughout our lives. We grow, learn to talk, learn to drive, and lose our car keys—but we never get more neurons. How we use those neurons gets much more sophisticated with age, as we will delve into later, but the sheer number is stable.

Whether male or female, our brains develop in the same order. When we are born, our brains are not fully operational. Some people have argued that baby humans are born with underdeveloped brains because of evolution.[3] Briefly, because we stand upright, our pelvis isn't very wide and not the best posture for delivering big-brained babies. To successfully deliver babies, we have to have babies with smaller heads, just to get them out. Granted, I would have slapped anyone telling me this after I delivered a seemingly enormous Maya, but it does make sense. So we deliver babies with smaller heads, but those heads need to eventually house large, complex, intricate brains (another perk of our evolution). So babies have to come out a little underdone. Once they get out, they finish cooking.

Think of the brain and its development as a pyramid:

- At the bottom of the pyramid is the brainstem, which is topped by the midbrain. This part of the brain helps us live in the most basic ways, controlling bodily functions like breathing and blood pressure. This is all newborns really have online and ready to go at birth, and why they spend most of their time doing the basics like eating and sleeping.

- Next up the pyramid is the limbic system. This includes the hippocampus, amygdala, and hypothalamus and helps with learning, memory, and controlling emotions. Your newborn sucks at memory and emotion regulation, right? That is because the limbic system is still developing, becoming fully functional during childhood.

- At the top of the pyramid is the prefrontal cortex. This part of the brain controls higher-level thinking, like logic and planning. It helps us differentiate right from wrong, strategize for a raise at work by selling more widgets and not telling our boss off, and figure out the appropriate punishment for our misbehaving child. Talk to children in middle school. They don't yet have a fully formed prefrontal cortex. This part develops last, well into adolescence.

What determines this common brain development? Our genes code for the development of these brain structures. And boys and girls have 99.8 percent of their genes in common. Keep in mind that we share about 99 percent of our genes with chimps and mice and 85 percent of our genes with zebrafish (we even share 15 percent of our genes with mustard grass). This means that only 0.2 percent of all our genetic material can explain all the differences between males and females. And that 0.2 percent difference has to include all of the obvious biological and physical sex differences, like genitalia and height differences.

## What Are the Differences?

At conception, depending on which sex-typed chromosome a dad contributed, the fetus has either two X chromosomes or an X and a Y chromosome. The Y chromosome (or rather, one tiny gene on the short arm of the Y chromosome) triggers the development of the testes, which in turn starts secreting testosterone just six weeks after conception. The testosterone (along with anti-Mullerian hormone) turns the fetus into the boy we recognize, with the correct parts inside and out. If the Y chromosome isn't present, it can't override an important gene on the X chromosome (called DAX1) that signals the body to create ovaries. Without that override and the testes to produce testosterone, the fetus develops into a girl, with ovaries that produce estrogen. Most parents don't know that baby girls and boys are born with the same amount of testosterone. Boys simply experience an important four-month surge of testosterone (ending in the second trimester) that is critical to developing their genitalia. Everyone is exposed to and protected from estrogen in the womb (mom's hormones also peak). After birth, for about one to two months, boys get a second surge of testosterone and girls get a surge of estrogen (referred to as mini-puberty). If there are any biological differences in the brains of boys and girls, this is when it most likely happens—but that if is controversial. From about four months of age until puberty, boys and girls don't differ in their levels of testosterone, estrogen, and other sex-related hormones. So please correct parents who blame their seven-year-old son's crazy behavior on testosterone. Until puberty, his testosterone level doesn't differ from that of girls.

So there are some genetic differences, although not much, and there are some hormonal differences between boys and girls. The hormonal differences aren't apparent during childhood, but they are different during some important developmental periods. These hormone surges during development have led some to argue for differences in the brain development of boys and girls.

## PINK BRAINS, BLUE BRAINS

In 1959, W. C. Young, a founder of behavioral neuroendocrinology, along with his trainees Charles Phoenix, Robert Goy, and Arnold Gerall, wrote an influential paper that was published in the journal *Endocrinology*. They had been conducting research on guinea pigs and found that early doses of testosterone influenced adult guinea pigs' mating behavior. If baby female guinea pigs were given a shot of testosterone, they were more likely to act like males when it came time to mate (although this refers to mounting behaviors, I personally imagine female guinea pigs sidling up alongside a male and saying, "Hey baby, what's your sign?"). Based on these animal studies, Young and colleagues concluded that sex-specific hormones had actually altered brain tissue, not just the gonadal tissue. The hypothesis, referred to as the organizational-activational hypothesis, basically argued that sex hormones affect the brain, which in turn affects behavior.[4] Although this was based on animal models and focused on sexual mating behaviors, others have used this basic premise to explain all sorts of other behaviors in humans. The rationale that hormones lead to permanent differences in the brains of boys and girls is a direct descendent of the female guinea pig with smooth moves.

The pink brain/blue brain argument of today, especially as it relates to children, is most loudly heralded by author Michael Gurian and psychologist Leonard Sax. Both argue that boys and girls have starkly different brains, which leads to differences in behavior and learning styles.[5] Along with Simon Baron-Cohen (author of *The Essential Difference*) and Louann Brizendine (author of *The Female Brain and The Male Brain*), they argue that there are three types of brain-based gender differences—in brain structure, brain function, and hormones.[6] Let me detail the most popular example from each of these three domains.

## Corpus Callosum

It is widely reported that males and females differ in the size of their corpus callosum, the bundle of fibers that connects the left and right hemispheres of the brain. Gurian, in *Boys and Girls Learn Differently!*, states that females have a larger corpus callosum than males (up to 20 percent larger). This has been a popular idea since a study was published in 1982 and caught the attention of TV talk show host Phil Donahue.[7] Donahue claimed this difference was the basis for women's intuition, and that remark was picked up by *Time* and *Newsweek*. "Gurian argues that girls' larger corpus callosum allows for more cross-talk between hemispheres (although what that really means is unclear).

There are three tiny problems:

1. The study was based on only five female and eight male subjects.

2. Two review articles, a 1997 meta-analysis of forty-nine research studies (by psychologists Katherine Bishop and Douglas Wahlsten[8]) and a 2009 review of post-mortem and brain imaging studies (by Mikkel Wallentin), found zero differences between the relative

size of the corpus callosum between genders.[9] As Wallentin concluded, "The alleged sex-related corpus callosum size difference is
a myth." So, what filtered into the popular culture was based on
one study (picked up by Donahue) that has now been completely
refuted.

3. Importantly, neuroscientists looking at a brain can't tell whether
it belongs to a man or a woman.

The assertion about the size of the corpus callosum is related to the
assertion that men have more lateralized brains than women, meaning
that men only think with one side of their brain at a time. This is trans-
lated into the popular belief that women multitask better (this is why
women are supposedly better at calling the doctor's office, cleaning the
kitchen, and helping with homework simultaneously). Here's the reality:
a meta-analysis by Iris Sommer and colleagues conducted in 2008
found no evidence of greater lateralization for men than for women.[10]

## Brain Function

There are supposed differences in how pink brains and blue brains
function. For example, Baron-Cohen, in his popular 2004 book *The
Essential Difference*, argues that the female brain is hardwired for
empathy and the male brain is hardwired for understanding and
building systems. He claims this is due to exposure to testosterone
in the womb. This assertion was in heavy rotation in popular media,
thanks in large part to Baron-Cohen's related argument that autism is
just an exaggerated male brain that can make no connections to the
social world.[11]

What is the basis for his argument that girls are empathizers and
boys are systemizers? One study: His graduate student, Jennifer Connellan, entered the hospital rooms of one hundred newborns and
showed the babies two stimuli—a dangling mobile and herself. The
researchers timed how long the babies looked at each stimuli and determined that the newborns preferred social objects if they looked longer

at the grad student and preferred mechanical objects if they looked longer at the mobile.[12]

The study had a major flaw, though. The graduate student—the person who was trying to find a sex difference and using herself as the social stimuli—was aware of the sex of the baby. Imagine these hospital rooms, with their pink or blue balloons, their pink or blue going-home clothes laid out, and the babies' names proudly displayed. There is a reason researchers are supposed to be blind to these details; when they know them, researchers can elicit the very behaviors they expect, even when they don't mean to (see more on this issue in chapter 9).

The size of the findings was also extremely small. Yes, girls looked at the mobile less than boys did. But when it came to looking at the student, the boys looked at her 46 percent of their total time and girls did 49 percent of their time. That is a very small difference between boys' and girls' interest in people. I personally wouldn't make a big claim about girls, but not boys, being born empathizers with only a 3 percent difference in their looking times.

## Hormones

Some researchers claim that pink brain/blue brain differences are due to hormones. Gurian, who most frequently cites *Brain Sex* by Anne Moir and David Jessel, argues that boys are better in math than girls because of hormones.[13] He states that boys' bodies receive daily surges of testosterone that boost their cognitive abilities, whereas girls can only really learn the few days a month when their estrogen is surging.[14] No study is provided for this claim, but he does include in his references "anecdotal confirmations, personal observations, and just good common sense", not to mention articles from *Reader's Digest*.

Many, many researchers, ranging from developmental and educational psychologists to neuroscientists, have refuted these pink brain/blue brain arguments. But my frustration is that these gendered arguments continue to float around popular culture, influencing how we think about boys and girls. Mark Liberman, professor of linguistics at the University of Pennsylvania, was so fed up with these arguments that he began to speak out on his popular blog, Language Log. He said that trying to correct the many "false assertions about sex differences" in *The Female Brain* "is a chore that is starting to make me feel like the circus clown that follows the elephant around the ring with a shovel."[15]

# HITCHES IN THE ARGUMENTS

The problems with the current arguments for broad, brain-based gender differences are much more deep-seated than specific flaws or misinterpretations of particular studies. There are three basic problems.

### First Problem: Testing Animals

We can't do any experiments directly on humans to test the influence of sex hormones on behavior. Say I want to study the influence of testosterone on aggression. I can't randomly select a group of boys, give half of them a shot of testosterone, the other half a placebo shot, and then see what happens (for example, do the boys with the hormone boost get into more fights?). Nor can I give girls' doses of testosterone to see whether that makes them as aggressive as boys. The ethics board at my university would freak out if I proposed that study, and I would never get a parent to consent to a study like that.

If you can't do this kind of experiment with people, and experiments are the only way to test the influence of sex hormones, researchers have to do the best they can. Some of them test their ideas on rats. In fact, most of today's testosterone research is done with rats. For example, have you heard of the finding that testosterone leads to aggression and the rough-and-tumble play of boys? That assertion is based on studies with rats.[16] Interestingly, those same studies on monkeys don't yield the same effects. But researchers talk about the rat pups as though they were the same as Little Jimmy at preschool.

# The Reason I Wrote This Book

It seems relevant here to explain why I decided to write this book. I am a full-time professor with teaching and research responsibilities and a mom of two young kids. I don't have a lot of free time lying around, and when I do, I would much rather spend time with my family than work. But in 2008 I had been asked by the ACLU to talk to parents in Breckinridge County, Kentucky, about the school board's current practice of segregating their public middle school into boys' classes and girls' classes. The middle school was convinced that Michael Gurian's approach to brain-based gender differences was the answer to their educational dilemmas.

So, like a good public speaker, I investigated exactly what they believed about brain-based differences, or more precisely, what they had been taught at the Gurian Institute. I was shocked by what was going on and by what parents were willing to accept in their children's public school. I immediately began buying neuroscience books on sex differences, starting with *Pink Brain, Blue Brain* by neuroscientist Lise Eliot. I spent several years immersed in this issue, looking at what schools were doing, what parents believed, and what science actually showed.

It became clear to me that there is a lot of solid science out there showing no substantial sex differences in the brain. But the smart, well-respected, and credentialed scientists weren't good at sound bites, going on the *Today Show*, or running for-profit parent-training sessions. They weren't good at boiling down the importance of effect sizes into a blog post or Tweet. They weren't, in the advertising sense, sexy enough. Instead, they presented their findings at peer-reviewed scientific conferences, some of which I attended, along with a very small audience of other researchers. As we say in the South, there was a lot of preaching to the choir. And parents, already obsessed with a pink and blue world, were latching on to the gender difference books, not realizing they should check the authors' sources.

Later, when I was asked to speak in my own city at a public symposium on diversity, I glanced at the program and noticed two teachers from my own school district were identifying themselves as "Gurian Institute trainers." I realized that the public school system

that was educating my own kids was now buying into these assertions that had been repeatedly refuted by actual neuroscientists. Sitting on the dais that day, I decided I needed to be as loud-mouthed
about the actual science as possible. The science was out there, but
no one was listening. And so this book idea was formed—my attempt
to talk directly to parents instead of presenting another boring talk
at another boring conference where it does no good for actual kids.

## Second Problem: Brain Plasticity

The brain is easily shaped by environment and experiences (I will discuss how that works in a minute). Experiences include the sounds that
filter through your abdominal and uterine walls to be picked up by
your gestating baby to the way you soothe your newborn to sleep at
night. And these experiences affect the hardwiring of the brain. The
brain was designed from day one to be this way; it is how babies adapt
to whatever culture they are born into. Brains are so malleable and,
therefore, so variable, that it is difficult to conceptualize an "average"
boy brain or an "average" girl brain. That is likely why most of the brain
studies reported in the media are never replicated. Researchers didn't
do bad research; they are simply studying the most complex machine
in the history of the world, one that changes every second in ways
far beyond our understanding. This is a real problem if you are trying to make arguments about innate, inborn differences, made all the
more difficult by studying adults, which is far, far more common than
studying children or infants.

## Third Problem: Reverse Inference

Reverse inference is a broad problem for much of neuroscience
research. In other words, we still have a lot of tails wagging a lot of
dogs. Let's take a look at a well-replicated gender difference, such as
reading the emotions of others in adulthood. We put eight men and
eight women (a common study size) in an fMRI machine (see page 89).

We show them images of faces and measure the blood flow in the brain while they are looking at those faces. We then statistically compare the average blood flow in the brains of men versus women. If there is a significant difference in a few brain cells, any cells, then we say, "Aha! That region of the brain is responsible for reading emotions. And look: men and women do it differently!" See what happened here? We worked backward: men and women differ on a behavior, there is a difference in the brain, therefore innate brain differences caused the behavior difference. It is just as likely that girls were socialized to talk and think about emotions (remember chapter 4) much more than boys (who are told to buck up and remember that emotions are for sissies). Those differing experiences shaped their brains. The brain differences, then, are also a result of different behaviors, not just the cause of them.

There are a lot of other problems with making inferences in reverse. One is the heavy reliance on those statistically different brain scans. For example, if an individual shows statistically different blood flow (which is read as brain activity) in one region of the brain when looking at faces than when looking at houses, I infer that that specific region of the brain is designed for face processing. I ignore that other regions of the brain also seem active because I am only focusing on where a statistical difference pops up between the two scans. I am putting a lot of eggs in my one statistical basket.

This is a mistake, at least according to psychologists at the University of California, Santa Barbara. Craig Bennett and colleagues, clearly trying to prove a point, put an individual in the fMRI, showed the individual a photo of a person and asked what emotion the person was experiencing.[17] They then compared the brain activity while looking at the face to the brain activity while looking at nothing (while "at rest"). This is a common technique to look for gender differences. The researchers found a significant brain activity difference in one region of the brain when looking at the face compared to when the brain was at rest. Should they make grand conclusions about face processing? No.

How does this study point out that bold inferences can be the result of accidental, spurious findings? The "individual" in the fMRI was a dead Atlantic salmon! Yes, a dead fish had enough random electrical brain activity while a face was displayed in front of it to equal the differences between men and women in a gender difference study (apparently, there is considerable random electrical firing that occurs in the brain right after death). Alert the media.

## REAL, RELIABLE DIFFERENCES

There are, however, some real differences between the brains of boys and girls. Here I focus simply on children. As Lise Eliot states in *Pink Brain, Blue Brain*, "overall, boys' and girls' brains are remarkably alike. Just as boys' and girls' bodies start out more androgynous than they end up in adulthood, their brains appear to be less sexually differentiated than adult men's and women's."[18] If we want to know how to help our own children be the best they can be, we need to know what is innate and what they are capable of. I care more about the brain of a child than about the brain of a forty-year-old man versus that of a forty-year-old woman, or the brain of a rat pup or a dead Atlantic salmon. What are boys' and girls' brains like, and what does that mean for raising them?

There are four differences that well-respected neuroscientists point out are reliable, replicated, and stable:

1. Boys and girls have different brain sizes. The old seed-measurers were right. Boys' brains are 8 to 11 percent bigger than girls' brains. However, this difference is similar in magnitude to the gender differences in height and weight of adults. Although girls have smaller brains than boys, girls have more gray matter—the actual nerve cells—relative to white matter than boys. Their brains are also more wrinkled, so more stuff gets packed into a smaller area. Boys have more cerebrospinal fluid, which helps buffer against brain injuries but also takes up space. So girls have

smaller brains, but they offset it by having more neurons packed in there. It all seems to even out. Because of these other differences, size difference, despite the common belief 150 years ago, is not related to anything except, I guess, hat size!

2. There is a difference in timing of development, and it is an important one for kids. Around the time of puberty, girls finish their brain development. This happens one to two years earlier than boys and is similar to physical development, in that girls usually begin puberty one to two years earlier than boys. For much of brain development, as with physical development, girls are a step ahead of boys. Remember from chapter 4 that girls develop language skills a few months before boys, but the difference largely goes away later. So if I measure nine-month-olds on some cognitive task, the girls may outperform the boys. And if I measure ten-year-olds, the girls may have different brain activation than the boys. But this does not necessarily indicate innate gender differences in the brain. It simply means that I took snapshots of boys' and girls' development that captured different phases of that development. It is like having a race between a boy and a girl to see who runs fastest. Suppose their speed is exactly the same, but the girl takes off one minute before the boy; my snapshot at the finish line shows the girl crossing first, but that tells me nothing about who runs faster. Developing at different rates does not shed light on adult abilities. (You can correct the parent who brags that his child started talking earlier than yours; it doesn't predict anything.)

3. The only reliable structural difference between boys' brains and girls' brains is a tiny cluster of cells in the hypothalamus (specifically, the third interstitial nucleus of the anterior hypothalamus, or INAH3), which is an area that controls a lot of metabolic functions, and is about the only area consistently shown to be influenced by testosterone. According to Rebecca Jordan-Young, a sociomedical scientist at Barnard College, no one really knows what this specific

area does yet, but it may be responsible for clearly sex-differentiated physiological processes, such as menstruation.[19]

4. There may be some differences in toy preferences due to hormones. I include this here because this isn't based on rat studies, as discussed above. Sometimes nature provides the experiment. Very rarely, but often enough to be studied, girls are born as genetic females but have high levels of testosterone. They have a complicated disorder called congenital adrenal hyperplasia (CAH). This is as close to an experiment as we can get. We can compare girls with CAH (who have "boy levels" of testosterone) to those girls who don't have the disorder (who have "girl levels" of testosterone). Eight independent studies looked at the toy and game preferences among girls with CAH, and seven of the eight studies found that girls with CAH were more likely to select boy toys for play than were the other group of girls.[20] Despite all the things blamed on testosterone, they didn't play more rough-and-tumble and they weren't more aggressive than typical girls. They also didn't want to play with boys or have masculine occupations. In other words, these results seem to apply only to toy play: if you give girls a bunch of testosterone, it doesn't do much except make them like cars more. Even this noncontroversial finding (seven of eight studies agree, which is miraculous in the world of neuroscience of gender) needs to be taken with a grain of salt. For example, when you actually look at the data, you get a slightly different picture. Researchers measured the amount of time the girls with CAH versus typical girls played with feminine toys (such as tea sets, Barbie dolls, and baby dolls) and masculine toys (such as a garage with cars, a bus, X-Men, and Lincoln Logs). While girls with testosterone played with the boy toys longer than typical girls did (633 seconds versus 420 seconds), all girls played with the boy toys longer than the girl toys. Even the typical girls, with their "girl" levels of testosterone, played with the garage and cars three times longer and with the Lincoln Logs six times longer

than with the baby doll! In fact, everyone's number one favorite toy was Lincoln Logs. The number two favorite for everyone was the garage and car. The two groups of girls did not differ in favoring the boy toys, regardless of hormone levels.[21]

What about other differences in the behaviors of boys and girls (many of which were discussed in chapter 4)? I don't really know, and neither do people who study sex differences in the brain for a living. Geert DeVries, the director of the Center for Neuroendocrine Studies at the University of Massachusetts-Amherst, specializes in sex differences and has said, "Despite decades of research, we still do not know the functional significance of most sex differences in the brain."[22] This is echoed by Melissa Hines, a neuroscientist at the University of Cambridge: "Sex differences in cognitive ability have not been clearly linked to either organizational or activational effects of hormones."[23]

Yes, there are differences between boys and girls. But those differences are much smaller than reported in the popular media, and we have no idea what exactly those differences mean for actual boys and girls. We do know that your job as a parent is critical. Experiences make all the difference.

## HOW EXPERIENCES SHAPE THE BRAIN

If studies that look at brain or hormonal differences in adults tell us nothing about hardwired differences, how do we know which differences are innate and which are due to learning about the world through the lens of gender?

I mentioned earlier that babies are born with all of the neurons they will ever have. Those neurons, however, are not connected to one another. Neuroscientists use this analogy: Everyone has phones, but none of those phones have lines in or out. It's important to have the hardware, but until phones are connected to other phones, they are not much use. The goal of development is to connect the phones.

What exactly happens? Each neuron in a baby's brain has an output wire, an axon. The neuron sends out information (in the form of electrical and chemical signals) on this single axon to other neurons, which pick up the message on their input wires, called dendrites. Each neuron has thousands of these input wires, which become densely branched over time, like an old tree. In fact, babies grow 83 percent of their dendrites after they are born. No wonder they sleep so much (I wasn't kidding when I said they come out underdone). By the time your baby is three, each axon sends out information that can be picked up by fifteen thousand different neurons.

A synapse is where an axon (for output) connects with another neuron's dendrite (for input). In the first ten years of a child's life, they form trillions of these synapses. They are like a very intricate chain of dominoes. One neuron connects to another, which connects to another, which connects to another (and remember, we are born with one hundred billion neurons). So activating one neuron can trigger the activation of another neuron, which triggers another, and so on. This is why the smell of gasoline reminds me of my grandfather's auto body shop and why hearing a Steve Miller song reminds me of spring break in 1993. I have created trillions of synapses, or connections, over the course of my life that are entirely unique to me.

Here is where it gets interesting. Between two months gestation (while you still feel nauseous) and two years old, babies form 1.8 million synapses per second. But that doesn't mean they are useful connections; most of them are simply random synapses between neurons. Each neuron just reaches out and connects with any dendrite it can find and rapidly creates dendrites every second.

At first, because of this rapid growth, there are far too many connections. An updated phone analogy (most kids wouldn't even recognize a phone line these days) is to think of social networking. Think of a fourteen-year-old on Facebook who has made connections with every possible person she has ever met and every possible person her friends have ever met. If a random stranger sends her a "Friend Request," she gladly accepts. She collects thousands and thousands of "Friends," regardless of her association with them. She is like the toddler with far too many synapses. As her parent, you partially helped her create so many connections. You set up the account and helped her link up with all your relatives. You played a role in helping the connections start, but much of it was beyond your control. The infant and toddler will be creating millions of synapses no matter what.

But the brain doesn't need that many synapses. In fact, too many synapses drain energy from the useful ones. So, our brains eliminate the ones that aren't useful. Specifically, when a baby's brain fires up a neuron, electrical energy goes through the axon and connects up with a dendrite. The molecules involved actually change and make the synapse more stable. The more electrical currents there are (in other words, the more a synapse is used), the more stable and strong it becomes. But, if a connection doesn't get used, it literally disappears. It's like the fourteen-year-old is growing up a bit and sorting through her Facebook account to defriend all of the people who aren't actually her friends.

It is truly a case of "Use it or lose it." Parents often underestimate the power they have to make lasting, neurological changes in their children's brains. This is a parent's number one job: make sure your kids make and keep valuable connections because once a synapse is lost, the related ability is lost forever. Here are two examples:

- One lesson in how early experiences shape the brain comes from babies born with cataracts. This only affects about two hundred babies every year, but when it does happen, it is crucial for the baby to have cataract-removal surgery within the first couple of months after birth. If not, the baby may never develop sight in that eye. During the first two or three months of life, the neurons used for vision are busily sending visual messages from each eye to the brain (as my old graduate school professor who studied vision used to say, "We see with our brains, not our eyes"). If no visual messages go through, the neurons dedicated for that purpose wither and die. Even if the cataract is removed at eighteen months, the synapses meant to do the job have already packed up their bags and left town. Those early visual experiences make permanent changes to the brain that can't be compensated for later.[24]

- A more common example—one that has affected you and your kids—concerns our ability to produce language. When your children were born, they could hear every sound in every language. Those synapses that helped in that process formed quickly. Makes sense, right? As a baby, I don't know what language my mom and dad are going to speak. I need to be able to hear all the sounds, whether it is Mandarin Chinese, Dutch, English, or the click-based Khoisan languages of Africa. But if I am not exposed to that language in my daily life, I will permanently lose the ability to hear that sound because the synapses that don't get used wither away. By about ten months, babies can only hear the sounds in their native language. For example, by a year old, babies who only hear English can't hear important distinctions in Mandarin Chinese. And similarly, babies who only hear Mandarin can't hear certain English sounds that don't occur in their language (such as the "r" sound). If you wonder why it is hard to learn a foreign language in adulthood, it's because we lose the needed hardware, that is, the unneeded synaptic connections.

Children have a large number of synapses until about age eight or nine. Between early childhood and adolescence, they lose twenty billion synapses per day—the ones that don't get used. These are permanent losses, never to be regained. This is why it is hard to teach an old dog new tricks (an old chestnut confirmed by science). The old dog just has fewer synapses, and it becomes increasingly difficult to grow new ones.

# WHAT'S A PARENT TO DO?

It is important to help strengthen our children's important synapses so that they don't get eliminated. That isn't nearly as tricky or technical as it sounds. Start by not limiting what toys and play activities your child is exposed to simply because of gender. If you eliminate half the possible experiences based on gender, kids lose the ability to do all they were born capable of doing.

Let's assume you think having good spatial abilities is important. It is, by the way, if you want your child to excel in geometry, be placed in advanced math classes, and do well on the standardized tests often required to get into college. It's also key to reading maps and not getting lost. Boys excel at spatial tasks compared to girls, in part, because they spent a childhood playing with blocks, Legos, and Lincoln Logs (experimental studies have shown this link).[25] The important synapses that help with those skills were strengthened by use during play, more commonly called learning. By the time boys need to take standardized tests to qualify for math scholarships, those synapses are well formed. Girls, however, have no traditional toys that foster spatial skills— none. Girls are not traditionally given blocks, Legos, or building toys. Why would we expect them to have those connections ready to go when we never helped strengthen them?

What about the importance of empathy? It doesn't show up on a standardized test, but it helps us read the facial cues of our friends and know they are sad. It helps us comfort our disappointed children after they weren't picked for the baseball team. Boys get shortchanged in the world of empathy development. For all the talk about brain-based differences in boys and girls, it is rarely discussed that boys like dolls just as much as girls until after their first birthday. Boys are just as hardwired to connect to others. Remembering the "big" study claiming girls are born empathizers and boys are not, the reality was that boys spent 46 percent of their time compared to girls' 49 percent of their time looking at a person. But, in general, we don't buy dolls for boys and we don't foster caretaking. We don't encourage, or sometimes even allow, boys to talk about their feelings or express a full range of emotion. Those synapses, the ones most connected with processing the emotional needs of others, don't get strengthened as much as they do for girls. By the time they are in their thirties, permanent changes have taken place in their brains that lead them to process the emotions of others differently than do women (and perhaps not as adaptively). [26]

As I hope is apparent in this book, my advice isn't about raising gender-neutral children. I don't even find the term *gender neutral* very meaningful or clear. My parenting advice is to raise children in a way that preserves all the potential connections they are born with—the ones that help them understand mechanical objects, express emotions verbally, do calculus, read fluently, control impulsive risk-taking, and so on. All of these skills are dependent on keeping important synapses in place and active.

Here are some suggestions for taking advantage of the malleability of the brain. These aren't divided by gender; they are important, regardless of gender:

- Talk, talk, talk about objects, people, and animals you see, events that happened yesterday, people you know, and feelings you feel. Narrate what you are doing as you are doing it. Language skills are socially and academically critical. These connections only develop with input from you (TV doesn't work the same way).

- Be responsive to emotional expressions. When babies and small children are sad or scared, help comfort them. Importantly, help them label the feeling. "That dog scared you, didn't he?" As children get older, their emotions get more complex. But it's crucial to talk about all of them. Being able to recognize and distinguish between disappointment, jealousy, embarrassment, anger, fear, sadness and happiness, contentment, and anticipation is essential for later emotion regulation.

- When your baby makes sounds, respond. She doesn't need to articulate words yet to have a conversation. When he coos, say, "Oh, do you like your blanket (or whatever he is looking at)?" Learning the basics of conversations—I say something, then you say something—is important for learning both social and language skills.

- Be sensitive to emotional distress. Babies should not be left to cry it out. It doesn't toughen them up. Babies left to cry for long periods of time develop strong synaptic connections relating to negative emotions.[27] Remember, if the brain experiences something repeatedly, it gets stronger. Also, being responsive to their distress helps babies develop strong, positive attachments with you, not the clingy, whiny kind of attachment. A warm attachment tells your baby that you are there for him, that she is important, and that when he needs you, you have his back. Babies and children with strong attachments with their parents are braver, less whiny, and more likely to thrive independently in the world. These lessons from infancy stay through adulthood.

- Encourage physical activity. Babies shouldn't be confined to one spot, even when they are complacent and able to sit in their bouncer for hours on end. Encourage young children to move, crawl, and walk. Roll balls back and forth. Being encouraged to move and play actively helps develop motor neurons and strengthens the synapses that help with hand-eye coordination. As children get older, switch the television off and force them to actively play on swings and bikes and with balls. This means setting rules about electronic devices, which seem to be hypnotic for kids.

- Read every night. This not only models the importance of books but also contributes to the language input that is so crucial. This is important for infants as well as older children. I read four or five board books to Grace every single night before bed. I then read to Maya every night, even at her age (nine). It has become a sweet bonding time.

- If you speak a second language, speak to your child in that language from birth. By their first birthday, they will have lost much of their ability to pick up a second language. Don't worry that the two languages will be confusing. Kids figure it out.

- Wrestle and snuggle. Both types of physical interaction are important. Wrestling and rough-and-tumble play help develop gross motor skills. Sometimes, at my house, this comes in the form of the tickle monster who attacks small children. Snuggling, that close affectionate warm embrace, helps develop the emotional bonds that all children need with the adults in their lives. This close physical bonding helps soothe anxiety, strengthens social skills, and improves later relationships.

- Practice letter sounds and ABCs with preschoolers. Early reading skills are important to develop during preschool and can often be the focus of games. For example, we call out letters we see on street signs. Reading is an extremely complicated cognitive task, and children need all possible synapses to help out. As children get older, encourage writing. Being able to express thoughts with language is an entirely different, yet highly complex process that needs constant reinforcement. Buy your child a journal to write in. This helps writing skills, reading skills, and emotional development.

- Have a pet. Taking care of others is the best way to nurture children's ability to nurture. Hate animals? Get a hermit crab or a goldfish from the mall. Anything that needs care and love will help.

- Play sports. Ball sports are extremely important for developing hand-eye coordination. It also helps spatial skills (imagining a ball traveling through space is an important part of spatial awareness). Playing sports also helps overall gross motor skills. It encourages teamwork, which helps build social skills. Maya is no hard-core athlete, but there are plenty of sports teams for her that focus more on skill building than score keeping.

- Have baby dolls available. We want all kids to grow up to be nurturing. These are skills that develop over time. For parents who don't think their son wants a pink doll, there are boy dolls in overalls and blue jeans. Stuffed animals also work. The details don't matter. What matters is the caretaking play. For kids who hurl their dolls through space to see how hard they crash into the wall, fostering nurturance may have to be more explicit. If you want your kids to grow into parents who know how euphoric their own child's embrace can be, help them learn those skills now.

- Have puzzles, mazes, and building toys available. Remember that Lincoln Logs were the favorite toy of all the kids in the study I described earlier. This type of play is critical for developing spatial skills and mental rotation tasks. Legos are now marketed to girls as well as boys, so there are now varieties to suit a range of tastes. Work on building projects. Home improvement stores (such as Home Depot and Lowes) usually have workshops every Saturday for kids. Take your kids. Or build a birdhouse or a jewelry box from a woodworking kit. These activities help develop mechanical skills.

- Avoid guns and violent games. The skills that are used frequently are strengthened. You probably don't want violence to be the skill that gets the most use.

## THE FINAL FOUR:
## WHAT ARE THE KEY ISSUES?

- Most of the claims about brain and hormonal differences between boys and girls are flawed, overstated, or based on rats. But they are mediagenic!

- There are four reliable differences between boys and girls: brain size, rate of brain development, size of the third nucleus of the anterior hypothalamus, and the degree of interest in mechanical toys.

- Enormous amounts of brain growth and development take place across childhood, not becoming complete until adolescence.

- If skills and abilities don't get used, children permanently lose those abilities. Experiences determine which synapses stay and which ones disappear. Gender-blind parenting isn't about breaking gender stereotypes per se. It is about enabling your children to maintain as many cognitive, social, and emotional abilities as possible.

PART III

# RAISING UNIQUE
## (FUN, WELL-ROUNDED, SMARTER, AND HAPPIER)
# KIDS

# How Children Help Create the Differences We See

**At this point, I can boil down everything** from previous chapters into two main lessons:

1. Part I: We are obsessed with gender, in every situation, with every person, whether it is relevant or not. We seem to make everything about boys versus girls. This division is less about gender per se and more about fitting people neatly into a category. The problem is that children latch on to gender and make it an important, and limiting, part of their lives.

2. Part II: Constant use of gender to define and the repeated quoting of "innate gender differences" is simply misguided. It doesn't reflect actual gender differences or the accurate size of those gender differences (which are usually quite small). This matters because treating children differently can lead their brains to develop differently—in ways that permanently limit their capabilities.

In part III, I hope to teach a few more lessons, including how focusing on gender is not only misguided, but also harmful to your kids. For example, your daughter may think she is not good in math in seventh grade simply because you say "What a good girl!" every time she does something helpful. Your son may get in fights on the playground because people frequently told him that "Boys don't cry."

In this chapter, I discuss how children often create their own gender differences, such as differences in liking math or being aggressive, and how you can intervene before that happens. In chapters 8 and 9, I show how you may be parenting your son or daughter differently without even meaning to. We all grew up in a culture and are influenced by it in subtle ways. Trying to limit our own subtle gender stereotypes is tough for all of us (myself included), but as you will see, well worth the effort. In chapter 10, I discuss how gender stereotypes may be reducing your children's academic performance, even when you are trying to fight those stereotypes and even if your children don't believe the stereotypes. I give some proactive tips for helping your kids do their best at school. And in chapter 11, I explain how stereotypes are filtering down into the policies adopted by many public schools and why you should check into your own school's curricula.

## DR. SEUSS'S SNEETCHES

Dr. Seuss was a brilliant social psychologist. He knew the importance—and danger—of focusing too much on the groups we belong to. His Sneetches (from the 1961 children's story) were overly focused on whether they were plain-bellied or star-bellied. They decided that the presence or absence of stars on their bellies was indicative of many important differences. If you know the story, you know that "Those stars weren't so big. They were really so small. You might think such a thing wouldn't matter at all."[1] Sounds a lot like the small differences between boys and girls. But, as with gender, the Sneetches treated those small differences as vitally important ones. They segregated themselves, and with this separation, created much larger differences.

Kids aren't really any different than Dr. Seuss's Sneetches. They see a difference between two groups of people—a difference that everyone around them seems to be focusing on—and they take that difference and run with it. As I describe next, by preschool, kids only hang out with other kids in their same gender group. They create their own rules and enforce their own segregation. As Dr. Seuss says, "When the Star-Belly children went out to play ball, Could a Plain Belly get in the game? Not at all."[2] Check out kindergarteners at recess; as you will see, this kid-driven segregation leads to many of the later differences we see.

Only when the Sneetches couldn't tell who had stars and who didn't, did they realize that they were all basically the same, that "Sneetches are Sneetches." The problem with the analogy is that kids can't completely ignore gender. But perhaps the lesson for our kids should be that "kids are kids." Maybe we can help them realize that gender doesn't tell us much about a person.

How do children do all of this sorting on their own? You don't have to actively teach gender stereotypes for your kids to create and enforce them themselves. Our jobs as parents must be to help point out and correct gender stereotypes when we see them.

## LEARNING QUICKLY

When Maya was in preschool, her teachers turned birthdays into special occasions in the classroom. Each birthday child could invite a special guest to lunch that day and could bring in a favorite treasure from home to show the class. On Maya's fourth birthday, I was her special guest and I sat in a tiny chair at the tiny table and had lunch with her. After lunch, her class sat in a circle on the floor and Maya produced her two favorite toys from home to pass around the circle. Her favorite toys that day were an old rusty Matchbox car she had found buried in the backyard and a small plastic doll with plastic clothes you could take on and off.

The circle of preschoolers dutifully passed the toys around as Maya explained their significance (which consisted of basically "These are my toys, and I like them"). However, when a boy was next in line to handle the doll, he would lean as far back from the circle as possible, leaning so far back that his head was a few inches from the floor. He would force the girl to skip over him and hand the doll to the next available girl in line. Girls were just as subtle in refusing to handle the cars. The only girl to actually touch the car held it by the back left wheel, while her face registered disgust, as she flung the car at the next available boy.

After the first kid did this, I started really paying attention. Not one boy touched the doll and not one girl touched the car (except for the wheel flinger). It was like a force field surrounded the toys, repelling the touch of the wrong-gender child. It was clear that cars are for boys and dolls are for girls and all the children had gotten the memo. I am pretty sure that cooties were somehow involved.

This wasn't just an unusual sample of uncompromising kids with a hypervigilant fear of cooties. In fact, most kids are this rigid. Lisa Serbin, a professor of psychology at Concordia University, and her colleagues found that toddlers and preschoolers quickly learn the "rules" for each gender. Serbin's research with young children has repeatedly shown that all children start out preferring dolls to trucks. They all show the same interest in dolls, regardless of gender, until about eighteen months. Around the second birthday, though, things start to shift. Children start to show a sharp interest in same-gender toys, so girls are looking a lot longer at the doll and boys at the truck. Children at this age are also learning which activities, toys, and possessions "belong" to each group.[3] And they don't stop with the obvious stuff, either.

Serbin and her colleagues showed two-year-olds a series of pictures. The children would see an object, then hear a voice over a speaker saying, "This is the one I like. Can you look at me?" While the voice spoke, a man and a woman would appear on a television split screen placed in front of the toddler. Researchers recorded which person the toddler looked at. What they discovered is that children, by age two, knew the old-school male stereotypes. The toddlers knew to look at the man, and not the woman, when they saw hammers and fire trucks. But kids took it a step further. By age two, they also knew what researchers called *metaphorical stereotypes*. In other words, they also looked at the man when they saw bears and fir trees, but not when they saw hearts, dresses, tiaras, or cats. That is always surprising to me. Before children can use the potty, they associate bears with men and hearts with women. No one ever told them these things, but they still picked them up somewhere.

I always think that stereotypes are like the latest cold bug. You can use all the antibacterial hand sanitizer you want, but your kids are still going to catch it. Even when you try to shield your children from gender stereotypes, they are still going to pick them up somewhere. Like the cold bug, a lot of transmission comes from other kids.

What else do kids "know" about their gender groups? By the time they are three, they link girls with cooking, cleaning the house, wearing lipstick, and having eyelashes. They link boys with cars, climbing trees, fighting, and building things. By the time they are three, they also assume boys and girls have different personalities and traits. They assume boys are strong, big, fast, and loud, whereas girls are weak, little, soft, and quiet.

Children create these stereotypes at the drop of a hat. They learn one thing about one person and extend it to every boy or every girl. In one study, the researchers cleverly picked a preference that no one had ever linked with gender before, just to see how kids reacted. Children were told that a particular boy liked a sofa and a particular girl liked a table (not exactly trucks and dolls). Sure enough, kids ran with it. They then assumed that another, entirely different girl would also prefer a table to a sofa, whereas boys would continue to like sofas better.[4] Again, the lesson here is that children don't need adults to tell them about gender stereotypes. They are creating stereotypes based on the flimsiest of information.

Regardless of which qualities are associated with each gender, kids love their own group and think that their own group is best and everyone else sucks. In other words, boys love boys, and girls love girls. In my line of work, we call that in-group bias. Ask any child you know and you may hear some version of "Boys Rule, Girls Drool," or "Anything boys can do, girls can do better!" In many ways, this is a pretty psychologically healthy answer. You can't easily change your sex, so it helps to love the group you are born into. (I discuss what happens when your child doesn't love his or her gender group in the next chapter.)

## THE RIGHT STUFF

By preschool, children know all sorts of "rules" about their gender. They know their group, and they know what is right (and wrong) for their group. Remember, we have emphasized over and over to kids that their gender is important. They were, after all, immediately topped off with that pink or blue hat in the hospital. Kids want to fall in line. Above all else, they want to do what is right for their group. We see over and over again that children make choices based on what's right for their group more than any other criteria. The team matters more than the toy.

For example, children's toy choices are driven more by what they think fits with their group than even the actual toy. In multiple studies that have been replicated often, preschool children have been brought into a research lab and given a toy created by the researchers, one the children have never seen before. Some kids are told it is a toy that boys like to play with, and some are told it is something that girls like to play with. Boys who think they are playing with a boy toy think it is lots of fun. When they are told it is a girl toy, they say it is no fun and don't want it. Girls do the same thing. They love it when it is labeled a girl toy and dismiss it when it is labeled a boy toy. The toy never changed, just the label. It is not surprising, then, that girls make a beeline for the girls' section of the toy store and boys to the boys' section. It is often less about their interests and more about identifying with the "right" group.

Understanding this goes way beyond simply saying the "right" toy is more fun than the "wrong" toy. When children are given new toys and told they are either boy toys or girl toys, children explore the "right" toy more carefully, spending more time learning about it and figuring it out.[5] They touch it more, inspect it more, and ask more questions about it. Not surprisingly, they also remember more about those toys that were labeled for their group. Remember—these are preschoolers! This is not about boys being born to play with trucks and girls to play with dolls. This is about labeling trucks as boy toys and dolls as girl toys coupled with children knowing which toy they are supposed to play with (and which toy to avoid like the plague). They then, naturally, develop an expertise in their own group's toys.

Knowing which is the "right" toy can even influence how good children are at playing with it. Raymond Montemayor, a psychology professor at the Ohio State University, brought six- to eight-year-old children into his lab. He told them about his new throwing game called Mr. Munchie (which was really just a Canadian toy unknown to kids in the U.S. Midwest). To score points, children throw as many plastic marbles as they can into a clown's mouth in thirteen seconds. Some of the children were told the game was "for girls, like jacks." Other children were told that the game was "for boys, like basketball." Not only did children like the game better when it belonged to their group, but they also performed better when it was for their group. Girls tossed more marbles into the clown when they were told it was a girl game than when they were told it was a boy game. Boys were also more successful when they thought it was a boy game rather than a girl game.[6]

These studies tell us that before they start first grade, children know they are boys or girls and know all sorts of "rules" about boys and girls. They know which toys boys and girls play with, how boys and girls are supposed to act, and what kinds of jobs boys and girls grow up to have. More importantly, believing a toy or an activity is for boys rather than girls will determine who plays with it, who learns about it, and who is better at it. The label alone is enough to drive kids' behavior. Think this only happens in research studies? Just think about Toys "R" Us. It is brightly labeled with pink and blue signs. Kids, of course, only want to shop in the "right" section. It is less about the toy and more about the team.

## Research at Home: Ask Your Kids

Many of you at this point may be thinking, "There is no way my child thinks that boys are strong and girls are quiet. My child doesn't believe these gender stereotypes. I think boys and girls are equal and I have worked hard to raise my children without stereotypes. I even bought a freakin' parenting book about gender."

Welcome to my world. I work extremely hard at reducing stereotypes, and even my own kids say some crazy stuff about gender. As a developmental psychologist, I am always shocked by the stuff kids think. I recommend asking your kids what they think girls are like and what they think boys are like. With a little probing, you might be surprised by what your kids think about boys and girls. Ask them to describe a typical boy and to describe a typical girl. Ask what types of things boys are good at and what types of things girls are good at. The biggest feminist gender researcher I know had a daughter who told her, while driving past a construction site on the way to school, that only boys could drive bulldozers. She almost wrecked the car.

Kids pick up these ideas and also create them out of thin air without any input from us (like my other friend's daughter who said only boys like oysters). Sometimes, they create these ideas that run counter to everything we are trying to teach. You are just one voice in a cacophony of voices in our culture. You have to make sure your voice is the loudest and the most outspoken.

# GIRLS TO THE LEFT, BOYS TO THE RIGHT

As we know, one way in which children help create many of the gender differences we see is by doing only those things that are "right" for their group. A second way children do this is by hanging out and playing only with same-gender kids. By preschool, children segregate themselves into boys' groups and girls' groups. They then socialize themselves—girls in the ways of girls, and boys in the ways of boys. These processes lead to bigger and more cemented gender differences later in life (in chapters 10 and 11, I describe the harmful effects of having the school exacerbate all of this segregation).

By the time children are three, if given the choice, girls begin choosing to play with girls and boys begin choosing to play with boys. If the next-door neighbor is a boy, your daughter will want to play with him because she wants to play. Your son is perfectly happy playing with his female cousin at their grandparents' house. But if given an option, kids usually pick another kid from the same gender. This preference is really strong from preschool until middle school. Life is very much us versus them for young children.

At least at first, children choose such a segregated world, in part, because of differences in how they play. Remember that in preschool, girls are talking a bit better than boys and boys are a bit more active than girls. So they tend to gravitate toward the same kinds of play. At this age, the type of play is really important. Boys tend to prefer rougher, more active play, and girls tend to prefer quieter play. The kids, therefore, who want to play rough, play rough together, and the kids who want to play quietly play quietly together. Because it is more activity-based at this age, the more active girls will still approach the boys and want to play (boys are less likely to approach girls to play, regardless of their play styles).[7]

But this changes as the elementary school years begin, when even the more physically active girls choose to play with other girls instead of the boys (even though the boys' play most resembles theirs). Likewise, the calmer, quieter boys still choose to play rough games with the other boys, even though that isn't their favorite kind of play. By the time school starts, the group becomes more important than the type of play. See the theme here?

Children begin choosing a segregated world, much like the Sneetches, because of the group itself. How do we know this? Because when children learn gender labels (for example, when they can sort people into groups labeled "boys" and "girls"), their preference for playing with kids of the same gender increases.[8] Incidentally, children also expect to get approval from adults if they play with same-gender kids, but not if they play with other-gender kids.

This segregation into boy groups and girl groups leads to bigger gender differences later. How could it not? Boys play in big groups, in activities often decided by peers. Girls play in two- or three-person small groups, often in adult-directed activities. Girls get the chance to be more flexible and practice compromising because there are fewer people who have to agree to the activity. They get to engage in a wider variety of activities. Also, because girls are playing in small groups, the play can be more verbal. It is difficult to have a conversation while playing football. So girls, who start out a little more verbal than boys, play in small groups that foster and hone their verbal abilities. Girls also get to practice their relationship-building, intimacy-creating skills. It is easier to pay attention to your friend's social and emotional cues when you only have one person in front of you. It is easier to share details about your own emotional state when the person is clearly listening to you. Girls get better at the one-on-one socializing. What started as a small difference gets larger because they continue to socialize themselves. Girls, because they often play in adult-directed activities, also get better at listening to and complying with adults. This is largely why girls do better in school than boys, often because they sit and listen to the teacher more often.

For boys, play often involves running and ball-catching. What started as a small advantage in gross motor activity becomes bigger as boys develop better and better hand-eye coordination. They also build muscle mass with all this rough, physical play, getting stronger every year. Navigating balls that travel through space helps hone spatial and mental rotation skills. Because boys typically play farther away from adults than girls do, they also develop independence and negotiating tactics. To have their voice heard in a loud group of competing voices, boys also learn how to assert themselves, carrying this assertive speech into the rest of their lives.

In the same way immigrants acculturate into a world of fast food, celebrity worship, and big-box stores, children acculturate into their respective gender worlds. Girls get better at Girl-World, and boys get better at Boy-World. The more time preschool and kindergarten children hang out with only same-gender peers, the more rigid they get in their gender stereotypes and the more they devalue the other gender's traits.[9] Girls are not only better at living in Girl-World (which is verbal, emotional, and cooperative), but they also don't value the things in Boy-World. Boys not only excel at Boy-World (which is active, independent, and assertive), but they also don't think Girl-World holds anything of importance for them. What a shame! All children, regardless of gender, should be well socialized to be verbal, emotional, active, and independent, as well as cooperative or assertive as needed. But kids' own strict segregation ensures they only develop half of these traits.

By middle school, as puberty changes their priorities and they begin to get interested in one another again, they are like people meeting from two foreign lands who don't speak the same language. After twelve years of living and breathing in one specific isolated social world, boys and girls want to interact. But Boy-World and Girl-World only taught and valued one style of interaction. So even though boys and girls don't want to be segregated any longer (much to the horror of teenagers' parents), they have a difficult time interacting and meeting in the middle. It is as though boys are from Mars and girls are from Venus.

# PEER PRESSURE

Sheep get a pretty bad rap. We pick on them as though they are the only ones who follow others mindlessly. The reality is that we all do it. One of the most famous books in social psychology is *The Social Animal* by Elliot Aronson.[10] We are all social animals. Most everything we do is driven by the need to fit in with others (even though we don't like to admit it). This isn't a bad trait; it helps our society function more smoothly. The classic demonstration of this is to get into an elevator and turn around so you are facing the back. What happens when others get on the elevator? They also turn around and face the back. Kids are no different. Much of what they do is based on what their peers are doing or what they think their peers expect them to do. There is a reason most parents have, at some point, uttered, "If your friends jumped off a bridge, would you do it too?" The honest answer is usually "Yes." (And before you get too judgy, remember that you did it, too. I know I permed my already very curly hair in high school because it was the late '80s and everyone had a big-hair perm. I looked like a poodle, but I fit in, and that was the most important part.)

When it comes to being the right kind of boy or girl, kids do what they think others want. They are aware of what their peers expect of them, and this affects their choices. In a study with four- and six-year-old boys, boys were more likely to pick a boy toy if their peers were around. If they were by themselves, their toy choices were more random.[11] The peers didn't have to say anything. The mere presence of other kids was enough to guide the young boys' play into being more boylike.

When I was a new researcher studying gender stereotypes, a father of a young son asked me what he should do about Christmas. His son wanted one of those giant Barbie heads on a stand with long hair you could style. The son, who was about six years old, wanted to braid and brush and comb. The dad, who was doing his best to accept his son's uniqueness, didn't know whether he should indulge his son or whether buying the Barbie would set his son up for a lifetime of torment. I think he was also secretly concerned that playing with the Barbie head would turn his son into a gay hairdresser. Once Dad was assured that his son would be gay or straight regardless of what Santa brought, he decided to buy the Barbie but also a baseball bat and glove. When we asked him several months later how the toys had worked out, the dad was pleased. He said that his son loved the Barbie, but without prompting from anyone, kept it in his closet when his friends came over and brought out the boy toys.

To be clear, I don't think this is a great solution. It does highlight, however, how savvy children are about which types of play are acceptable around other kids. By age six, this boy knew that his friends wouldn't accept the Barbie head as an okay play choice. Frankly, that story makes me a little sad. I wish the young boy lived in a world where he felt comfortable enough to say, "Gosh, I love styling hair." But he didn't. And, most importantly, he knew it. He purposefully made himself more gender stereotypical just to fit in with his friends.

Succumbing to peer pressure doesn't have to be driven by children's actual friends. Kids try to conform and emulate their same-gender peers even if the other kids are total strangers. Children want a toy if a same-gender kid is playing with it and reject it if an opposite-gender kid is playing with it. A boy is more likely to play with a doll if he sees another boy playing with one than if he only sees girls playing with them. On the flip side, if he sees girls playing with trucks, he is more likely to reject them, because those particular trucks must be "girl trucks."

Ever wonder why your son doesn't want dolls, kitchen sets, or arts and crafts materials, or why your daughter doesn't want action figures or car tracks? Watch television commercials geared to children. Or look at the boxes that these toys are packaged in. Children pay close attention to who is playing with these toys. They flat-out reject toys that are being played with by other-gender kids and report wanting toys played with by same-gender kids. Television commercials are directly related to toy requests. If marketers ever showed a bunch of boys playing with My Little Ponies, boys would immediately want to play with them. This happened with Legos. The packaging and commercials showed girls playing with Legos and the colors changed from red and blue to pink and purple; Legos sales increased immediately.

## Boy-World Is a Strict Place

This research reflects a harsh reality for boys. Girls are more flexible than boys about what kinds of toys they can play with and how they can act. Girl-World is a much more open, accepting place than Boy-World. For example, girls play with boy toys much more often than boys play with girl toys. It is acceptable to be a tomboy—that isn't a derogatory term. Grown women often brag about having been tomboys as children. But boys can be brutally teased for doing anything girl-like. No man ever bragged about being a sissy, which is the closest comparable term. Girls are allowed to branch out, whereas peers in Boy-World strictly enforce the gender rules.

We can't forget that children live in their own social world, with consequences for being "too unique." As parents, we have to be mindful of the pressures on children, especially boys. As much as I hate gender stereotypes, I wouldn't want my kids to get teased at school for being atypical, especially when they are just trying to be themselves. For boys who are nontraditional, it is helpful to keep these pressures in mind. Parents have to walk a fine line between nurturing the individual (which, for many boys, means liking traditionally girl-style clothes or toys) and helping them cope with conformity pressures at school. If your son is nontraditional, let the teacher know to be on the lookout for possible bullying. Casually remind your son to let you know if he ever hears negative comments from others. Help provide a safe space at home where his unique qualities are a non-issue.

## Teen Gender Rules: Harmful and Hidden

Even though middle school and high school boys and girls want to hang out together, it doesn't mean they have stopped enforcing their own gender rules. They may no longer reject a child who is playing with the wrong toy, but they are still strict about boys' versus girls' roles in the world.

For boys, the ideal teen boy is strong, athletic, uninterested in academics, and interested in dating as many girls as possible. Any behavior that doesn't fit with the athletic, tough, heterosexual, masculine stereotype can elicit harassment from other teens. Many boys are called "gay" or "fag" or something similar on a regular basis. Anything they do that doesn't fit the stereotype can elicit taunting and harassment. God forbid they ever cry in front of others. This harassment is often chalked up to "boys being boys," but it shouldn't be. It is understandably upsetting for boys, regardless of their actual sexual orientation.[12]

For girls, the stereotypes that get enforced by their peers are more focused on their bodies. The "ideal" teen girl is attractive, thin, and sexy. Many parents would be shocked to know that 90 percent of middle school and high school girls experience sexual harassment at least once.[13] This includes unwanted sexual comments, being touched against their wishes, having their butts grabbed or their bra straps popped, having their body parts rated, and being shown naked or degrading pictures on their phones or online. This tells girls, without an adult ever having to, that their bodies are the most important thing about them and that they should look sexy all the time. Girls who are harassed by their peers are more likely to show early signs of eating disorders, are more likely to be anxious and depressed, and are more likely to avoid school.[14] When this kind of harassment happens frequently, girls learn that this is how boy-girl relationships are; they are more likely to later date males who are abusive.

Most teens are embarrassed to discuss peer harassment with their parents, so parents are often the last to know. Boys may be particularly embarrassed to tell their parents that they were called "gay" at school.

There are several steps parents can take to help their teens:

- Ask your teenage sons and daughters, starting in middle school, about these experiences. Even if it hasn't happened to them yet, it likely will. Asking about it tells kids that they can talk about it with you if it does happen. Simply talking about it with an adult helps minimize some of the negative feelings that emerge.

- If your child is being harassed at school, phone the principal immediately. Most schools have a zero tolerance policy for bullying, and that is what this is.

- Help your teen develop some assertive coping strategies for dealing with harassment. Help them learn what to say back to the other kid (even saying something like "Shut up" helps minimize some of the negative effects of harassment)

- Help your teen understand that the harassment is not his or her fault. Boys who are called "gay" because they are not good at sports do not need to change themselves. Learning that this harassment is due to gender stereotypes and not to a flaw of the individual kid is extremely important. Remind teens that it will get better once they graduate.

## A HARD FIGHT

As we can see, children have their own gender rules, often based on flimsy information. They enforce those rules among themselves, creating rigid boundaries around Boy-World and Girl-World. The direct result of all this activity is that children's knowledge of their own-gender stuff is much more extensive than their knowledge of other-gender stuff. Once this snowball starts, it quickly grows, largely exacerbated by children's own memory biases.

Think back to chapter 3 and the discussion of the mental tricks we do to maintain our favorite gender categories. Kids whip out the same mental tricks to maintain and strengthen their own stereotypes. First, children pay attention to and remember information associated with their own gender but forget information associated with the other gender. We all have really elaborate mental images of what it means to be our gender (this mental image is called a "gender schema," coined by Carol Martin, a developmental psychologist at Arizona State University[15]). So women have elaborate ideas, with a lot of details, about being female. This is why most women know a thing or two about taking care of babies, basic sewing and cooking, how to braid hair, and how to navigate a shopping mall. Even if they aren't into those things, they have likely picked up the information along the way. And men have elaborate, detailed ideas about being males. This is why most men know a thing or two about how to fix cars, who is the best NFL team this season, and how to grill a steak. They may not be macho sports nuts, but this information seems to filter in from somewhere.

In order to build these elaborate intricate ideas of our own group, we need to filter out and ignore all of the information for the other group. There is only so much space in our brains (and remember, we are pretty lazy thinkers). So we focus our energies on remembering information related to our team.

Not only do kids explore, inspect, and play with same-gender toys more than other-gender toys, but they also remember more information relevant to their own gender compared to information relevant to the other gender. For example, a meta-analysis shows that boys remember boy-labeled pictures, words, and toys better than girls do, and girls remember girl-labeled pictures, words, and toys better than boys do.[16] This is how they build up their knowledge base of what they need to do to be the typical man or typical woman, and how they disregard the knowledge that is irrelevant to them.

How does this play out in real life? Perhaps you bought your son a sewing kit. You are trying not to stereotype and you figured it would be helpful later in life if he knew how to sew. The first problem is that the box is pink and displays a picture of a girl sewing. This is sufficient to clearly label it as a girl toy. Right away, he is not interested in the kit and probably thinks it's stupid. He would do this no matter what the toy was. The second problem is that he would never allow his friends to see him using it. His friends would make fun of him "being a girl." The third problem is that, even if you force him to sit down with the sewing kit, he won't remember much about it. If it is a girl thing, then he won't waste his time remembering how to use it. Sure enough, because he never catches on, sewing stays a girl thing.

Girls are a little more flexible (remember, Girl-World is a bit more easygoing than Boy-World), but they are not exempt from their own biases. If your daughter is given an erector set, she will first notice the boys playing with it on the box. It might as well be labeled "Not for you" because that is how she will interpret it. She will automatically be less interested in it. Even if she isn't embarrassed to show her friends, her friends won't be interested in playing with it when they come over to play. She will never really figure the set out, never fully realize all she can build with it. It simply won't keep her attention long enough. Mechanical skills stay a boy thing, strengthening the stereotype even though you tried to fight it.

These two scenarios both started with a clear labeling of the toy being for girls or for boys. That is key. The group category drives most of the processes, knocking kids out of the game before they even start playing.

The second mental trick kids use to strengthen their stereotypes (besides only remembering information that fits their gender) is that they only remember information that confirms their stereotypes, not information that breaks the stereotype. Margaret Signorella and Lynn Liben, developmental psychologists at Pennsylvania State University, showed children pictures of men and women doing traditional jobs and nontraditional jobs. Children saw pictures of men as firefighters or sewing and women as nurses or directing traffic. Children were asked to remember as many of the pictures as possible.[17] What did the researchers find? First, the kids remembered the traditional jobs better than they did the nontraditional jobs. They remembered men being firefighters and women being nurses better than any of the other jobs. The kids also made important, systematic errors. If they saw a male nurse, they remembered him as a male doctor. Or they would switch genders and misremember the person as a female nurse.

This is why stereotypes don't correct themselves on their own. This is why fighting gender stereotypes is so very hard, and often unsuccessful. It is why you can't just buy nonstereotypical toys and hope your kids play with them. You can have a house full of dolls for your son, and he may never touch them. You can have a room full of trucks and trains, and your daughter may ignore them. This is also why you can't assume that your kids are immune just because your family is not stereotypical. Just because mom works and dad cooks, that doesn't exempt kids from developing stereotypes. It is like spraying your house with Lysol and then sending your kids to a school full of coughing peers. They are going to catch a cold. Also, just buying your daughter books about female scientists probably won't work. She won't remember the book's message about girls' equality in science the way you want her to. You can't assume because your son or daughter saw Hillary Clinton as secretary of state that they understand that women can hold positions of power. They also won't remember a dad pushing his baby's stroller through the park. You can't rely on kids to pay attention to this information and remember it correctly.

Let me save you some time. Assume your children hold gender stereotypes. Assume they won't remember all of the contradictory examples they see in their everyday life. With those assumptions in place, you simply have to be more proactive in helping your kids battle these stereotypes. Kids can't fix a problem they helped create.

## CORRECTING KIDS' STEREOTYPES

What's a conscientious parent to do? In chapters 8 and 9, I discuss how you can play offense against gender stereotypes, how you can tailor your own parenting to reduce stereotypes and maximize your children's potential. But gender stereotypes are so pervasive, coming from every nook and cranny of the world, that playing offense isn't enough. You also have to play defense. You have to correct them when you hear them, not just hope the stereotypes will go away on their own. In fact, gender stereotypes won't go away on their own; they just get stronger.

When your children are in preschool, the stereotypes they repeat may seem silly. They aren't worried about women not pursuing careers in mathematics and men feeling constrained from taking time off from work for their families. Preschoolers usually have idiosyncratic, concrete, and seemingly random gender stereotypes. The other day, Grace told me that girls have eyelashes and boys don't. She has also announced that girls drive red pick-up trucks. I have heard from pre-schoolers that boys jump high, boys like broccoli, and girls eat blueber-ries. These are in addition to the stereotypes about boys being strong, loud, aggressive, and fast, and girls being quiet and soft. These are also in addition to preschoolers thinking that all doctors and firefighters are men and all teachers and nurses are women. The cyelash thing I couldn't care less about; the doctor thing has me a little concerned.

So you have to correct every one of these proclamations, not because it matters who children think has eyelashes. You have to correct the either/or thinking that is implied in these statements. No one group of people does everything alike, not one. Not all boys do anything alike. Not all girls do anything alike. If you stop this either/or thinking about the small stuff, it is easier to stop the either/or thinking about the stuff that really matters.

How do I correct these statements with my own children? I don't turn it into a lecture or a major issue. I simply make two points, and I make these same two points every time. First, I point out that both genders do have whatever it is she has commented on. In this case, I told Grace, "Both boys and girls have eyelashes. Not just girls, but boys too." Second, I give a concrete example of someone breaking her stereotype. In this situation, I said, "Think about Daddy. He has very long eyelashes. Mommy's eyelashes are so short I have to add makeup to them." Clearly, she didn't remember the counterexample on her own (as

I said before, kids never do), so I pointed it out for her. That's it—period! Sometimes, instead of just saying both boys and girls do something, I phrase it in terms of the variability. When Maya announced that girls are neat and boys are messy, I told her, "Some girls are neat and some are messy. And some boys are neat and some are messy." Then the second point stays the same. "Think about Daddy. He is very neat."

Dad often works as a good counterexample to stereotypes in our house, because I can contrast Mom and Dad and they know enough details about him to make the example concrete. But having two parents of different genders is definitely not necessary to make this point. Concrete examples of people who don't fit the stereotype can be your children's friends at school, cousins, teachers, neighbors, grandparents, or even a character on a TV show. Some preschoolers say, "Boys are brave." I would respond, "Some boys are brave and some girls are brave. Think about Dora. She is brave when she stands up to Swiper the Sneaky Fox." Three sentences. That's all. (Also, don't assume that if you are a single parent or in a two-mom or two-dad house that you are exempt from all these stereotypes. Your kids picked them up, too.)

When your children are in elementary school, the stereotypes become a little more worrisome. Maya recently told me that "boys get into fights." Granted, boys are more likely to show unprovoked physical aggression than girls. But there are many, many boys who will never get in a fight in their lives. So I applied the same two rules: I pointed out the variability and I provided a counterexample. "Some boys do get in fights. But there are many boys who never fight and don't like fighting. Plus, some girls also get into fights. Remember when Maggie kicked that boy who was mean to her? That was a fight. And think about Millen. He would never get in a fight."

For boys, a common stereotype about girls is that "Girls can't play basketball (or can't throw or can't play MarioKart)." Negative stereotypes about girls being bad at sports are rampant among elementary school boys. I would make the same two points. "Well, some girls can't play basketball, but some boys also can't play basketball. And some girls are really good at basketball. Just look at Lisa Leslie. She can dunk."

I correct stereotypes, even when they paint my own kids in an unfavorable light. Thinking everyone who belongs to one group does the same thing is the problem. I correct Maya if she says, "Girls are nicer than boys." I know plenty of bratty girls and incredibly sweet boys.

Kids in elementary school are also at the age when boys and girls are often the enemy, full of those dreaded cooties. When Maya is invited to a girls' only party, or one of her male friends is having a boys' only party, or one of the kids mentions only wanting to play with their "own kind," I offer my two cents. In this situation, I often just say, "I think it is so much nicer when boys and girls can play together. Life is a lot more fun when there is a little variety." Again, it is the either/or (aka Mars/Venus) thinking that is the problem.

When your children are in middle and high school, the stereotypes can be subtler than for the younger kids. These adolescent stereotypes are often either embedded in a discussion of peer pressure or refer to the boy-girl relationships that accompany puberty. "All the girls wear shirts like this," "All the boys joke around like this," "No girl [eye-roll] takes computer science," "No self-respecting boy likes poetry." Here, I make the same two points, although the response can also be subtler. In adolescence, a lot of teens' stereotypes are about fitting in with what they think their friends expect. In many ways, it is an argument about giving in to peer pressure.

A friend of mine had a tenth-grade son who got in trouble at school for using foul language within earshot of a teacher. Guys are often pressured by peers to act tough, and he was falling into that stereotype. My friend was horrified, and her son's response was that "All guys talk that way." Her best retort was "Just because some guys talk to their friends like that doesn't mean all guys do. Guys who want to go to college and get jobs and be successful don't talk that way. Which is a better example of being a man: cussing or holding down a good job?" He seemed to get the message.

A common statement among teen girls is that "All guys are jerks" (this is usually uttered after a breakup). Boys may say that "All girls are just whiny and clingy." The best response is simply, "Not all guys are jerks. That one guy is a jerk, but there are plenty of nice ones out there." Or "I know your last girlfriend was pretty clingy, but not all girls are like that." The goal is to point out that there is too much variation among boys and girls to make any global statements.

## IDENTIFYING STEREOTYPES

Although you should correct every stereotype you hear your kids say, oftentimes they won't be the ones saying them. Adults have made hundreds of incredibly stereotypical statements in front of my kids, or worse, directly to them. Other times, I recognize that a stereotype is at work, although my own kids are oblivious. In both of these situations, I have to be a little more delicate. But I can't let the stereotypes slide. Just like I don't want an adult telling my kids the Earth is flat, because that would hinder them in science class, I don't want these adults passing along their stereotypes either.

When an adult makes a stereotypical statement to my children, I wait until the kids and I are alone and then I point out how the adult was wrong. This is a nuanced situation. I have to walk a fine line between teaching respect for adults, but also keeping inaccurate statements from influencing my children. Grandparents, teachers, and my childrens' friends' parents are frequent culprits. So are the elderly ladies at the grocery store. The comments of people over sixty are easily explained. A recent retiree told Maya and me at the grocery store, "It is so nice to have girls because they are so helpful with the shopping." After she walked away, I whispered to Maya, "In her day, boys didn't help much with shopping. But now things are different and boys are just as helpful as girls."

It is a little more difficult with people in our lives whom we are close to and care about. I never want to blatantly call a loved one wrong (even though they sometimes are). One close relative frequently says, "Boys are so rough," while stepping over my own wrestling daughters. When this happens, I wait until the kids and I are alone and then remind them, "I know she always says that boys are rough. But she forgets that girls can also be rough, and plenty of boys aren't so rough. So I just want you to remember that when she says that, she is forgetting about all the rough girls and quiet boys in the world."

You may think this isn't worth the time and energy. But I have also overheard adults tell my kids that boys are naturally better at math than girls, boys just don't understand babies, and it is more important for girls to be pretty than smart. Of course I don't want my kids, or any kids, to carry around those gems as facts. If I had sons, I would be especially vigilant about pointing out these errors. The stereotypes that impact boys are often more socially acceptable than those that impact girls, and people feel more free to share them. For example, boys are often told by other adults to be tough and not cry. Last summer, a family friend's eight-year-old son hurt his foot. A stranger told him to buck up and get over it because men don't cry. I whispered to the boy, "Plenty of men cry. That guy is just confused. Don't worry about it."

The last way I play defense against all the stereotypes that my kids pick up is to point them out, even when my kids are oblivious to them. Sometimes this means teaching about discrimination. Erica Weisgram, a developmental psychologist at the University of Wisconsin-Stevens Point, was interested in increasing girls' interest in science. This had been tried many times, but was rarely successful. She and Rebecca Bigler conducted an experiment where they taught girls some especially interesting topics in science. Half of the girls just heard about cool science facts (this is the usual attempt to interest girls in science). The other half of the girls heard the cool science facts but also heard about some of the negative stereotypes about girls in science and about how discrimination kept some women out of science careers.[18]

Were those girls discouraged by having stereotypes and discrimination pointed out? No. In fact, those were the girls who showed greater interest in science and felt more confident in their science abilities! Girls notice that few famous scientists are women. When they learn about scientists at school, they realize that women aren't often included. They don't need you to point that out. They get it. They know that girls aren't supposed to be physicists. No one has to tell them that. But, what they do need is someone to help them identify why. Although negative stereotypes and discrimination don't completely explain why so few women pursue science, they are a big part of the explanation. So point it out. Have the conversation.

You don't want children to explain the gender differences for themselves. Their own explanations are often very misguided. In one of Bigler's other studies, she asked girls why no women had been president of the United States. One-third of the girls thought it was against the law for a woman to be president. This was in 2007, not 1907.[19] When left on their own to explain the gender differences they see, their answers may not be in line with your values or reality.

Boys are even more constrained than girls by unspoken stereotypes. Boys often feel pressure to be tough and dismissive of authority figures, like teachers. A boy who is really compliant with the teacher is often teased at school. Boys are also never supposed to ask for help. Boys are doing academically worse in school than girls, across the school years, largely because the stereotype tells them to be tough, independent, and never ask for help.[20] The result of these constraints may be a son who doesn't pay much attention at school, and, when he struggles, doesn't ask for help. But studies have shown that boys who dismiss the old stereotypes—boys who are flexible in their notions of what boys and girls should be like—actually do better at school. So if you notice your son being influenced by this stereotype, if he gets in trouble at school or says disrespectful comments about his teacher, don't simply punish him. Also help him identify that there is a stereotype hidden in there and that, no matter the pressure, he doesn't need to go along with it.

Kids are important creators of their own stereotypes. They develop their own flawed opinions about boys and girls, ignore disconfirming information, and prefer to hang out with kids who are just like them, all of which further creates and reinforces stereotypes. As parents, much of our job is to play defense against the stereotypes that our children encounter. Correct the stereotypes you hear your kids say, point out when other adults are misguided, and discuss the negative stereotypes you see influencing your children. Sometimes the best offense is a good defense.

## THE FINAL FOUR: WHAT ARE THE KEY ISSUES?

- Children learn gender stereotypes very early in life. They take shreds of information and turn them into far-reaching stereotypes.

- Children are much more influenced by the "right" toys and peers than anything else. Girls only want to play with girl toys with other girls and boys only want to play with boy toys with other boys, regardless of the type of play. The gender-based "team" trumps everything.

- Children reinforce their own stereotypes by only hanging out with same-gender kids, socializing boys in the ways of Boy-World and girls in the ways of Girl-World. They also only remember information that fits their group and supports their stereotype.

- Because children form their own stereotypes, and those stereotypes are so difficult to change, parents need to correct the stereotypes they hear and point out the stereotypes they notice.

——— **CHAPTER 8** ———

# Parenting a Stereotype

**Several Christmases ago, we took Maya** and Grace to visit their grandparents. Grace, who was just beginning to show real interest in toys, was enraptured by the train set that went through the living room. She shrieked with delight, giggling and clapping her hands. She was so excited by the moving train with its whistle and flashing lights that she literally fell over laughing. A laughter-induced face plant is usually a good sign. The reaction was repeated the next week when we went to visit another set of grandparents. For almost an hour, Grace clapped, laughed, and stared at the moving train as it circled the track. All the other toys sat in a pile while her entire attention was focused on the train. The grandparents reveled in the moment, laughing at the baby's delight. Pictures were posted on Facebook.

When Christmas day arrived, it was time to open presents. Guess what Grace received for her first Christmas? Six dolls and a musical tea set. They were all fine gifts, picked out with love by doting loved ones. But not one present was based on her actual interests; they were all based on the stereotype of what she should want, as a girl.

Just knowing a particular child is a boy doesn't tell us how athletic he is or how good at math he is. Just knowing a child is a girl doesn't tell us about how sweet she is or how much she likes to talk. The moms of boys frequently tell me how nice it must be to have girls, who aren't as rough and disgusting as boys. I debate whether I should tell them Maya loves to sit on our laps, let one rip, and then laugh hysterically, or about the time at the restaurant we attracted stares as she belched the alphabet. If I tried to parent the stereotype of a girl, I would be missing the joy of parenting Maya. I would miss what makes my daughter unique, albeit kind of gross.

Unfortunately, many parents are influenced by whether they have sons or daughters. In a culture so obsessed with gender, starting at the first sign of a "baby bump," it is hard not to be affected by our preconceived notions of boys and girls. Likely (because you are human) you are influenced by stereotypes without knowing it. If so, those stereotypes influence how you parent your kids, which in turn influences how they develop. In this chapter, I first describe some of the common ways that parents treat their sons and daughters differently. As they say in AA, the first step is admitting you have a problem. Then I discuss why parenting a stereotype is not nearly as fun or fulfilling, for either the parent or the child, as raising a complicated and unique individual.

## PARENTING BOYS AND GIRLS

Very few parents ever make explicit statements to their children about what they can or cannot do because of their gender. Most parents, if I asked them, would firmly assert that boys and girls should be treated equally and would vehemently insist that they treat their sons and daughters equally. I believe the first but not the second part. Most parents think they treat their kids the same, because the differences in treatment are usually subtle and unintentional. The subtle shades of pink and blue are the hardest to detect.

So, yes, most parents believe that boys and girls should be treated equally. Indeed, a meta-analysis of 172 studies found no differences in how warm or restrictive parents are with their sons and daughters.[1] There are also no differences in how much parents encourage overall achievement in their kids. But, the reality is that by seeing our kids through the lens of gender, our parenting can be influenced by stereotypes, even accidentally and unintentionally.

## Parenting Babies

We are most prone to rely on stereotypes when our children are babies. It is difficult to pay attention to their unique qualities when they just lie there, cry, and drool. They don't show much interest in toys yet. They are primarily interested in milk and your dangling car keys. So we fill in the missing information about their personality and interests with stereotypes about what they should like. We don't know much about them as individuals, but we do know their gender. So we let gender drive a lot of our own behavior.

Not surprisingly, when researchers examined the rooms of infant boys and girls, they found differences in what babies are exposed to right from the start. Boys had more "toys of the world," like cars, trains, and machines; girls had more "toys of the home," like dolls and housekeeping toys.[2] Right from the start, parents are shaping whether their children will gravitate toward trucks or dolls once they become mobile.

Parents also differ in how they interact with their babies. Mothers talk more, interact more, and are more sensitive to the smiles of girl babies than boy babies. Baby boys are handled more roughly than baby girls. This is even true when the baby is a stranger in a research study and the researchers alternate whether they call the baby a boy or a girl. The "boy" gets handled like a boy, even when she is secretly a girl.[3]

## Parenting Older Children

As children get older, parents differ in how they handle the emotional lives of their sons and daughters. For example, parents talk about emotions, particularly sadness, more often with their daughters than their sons. When parents have the rare talk with their sons about emotions, it usually involves issues about anger or controlling their emotions. If something upsetting happens at school, parents are more likely to talk to a daughter about how she may feel sad, but talk to their son about just getting over it.[4]

Sons also get punished more than daughters, although parents are more tolerant of their sons' expressions of anger and physical aggression. And the boys know it. Sons, more than daughters, assume that they won't get into trouble with their parents for being aggressive.[5] Parents almost expect their sons to be aggressive. They try to teach them to control their emotions, yet allow for their "natural" aggression to be expressed. Daughters, however, know that if they feel angry, they will get in trouble for lashing out.

Parents also differ in what they expect sons and daughters to do at home. Sons are assigned to mow the lawn, take out the trash, and clean out the garage. They are also more encouraged to play on the computer, play and watch sports, and learn to build and fix things. Daughters are assigned to clean the house, set the table, and help with laundry. They are more encouraged than sons to read, take music lessons, and learn to cook.[6] It boils down to girls being encouraged to do "girl chores and hobbies" and boys being encouraged to do "boy chores and hobbies."

We see that parents, probably without meaning to, are socializing their children particularly in terms of emotional experience. Girls are allowed to be sad but not angry, and boys are allowed to be angry but not sad. Because of expectations about which emotions are okay for which kids, parents also have different expectations for their children's behavior. Boys are given greater leeway to express aggression than girls. This is reflected in the overwhelming availability of aggressive toys marketed to boys, such as fighting video games, guns, and war toys. I always wonder how children would develop if we didn't have these different expectations. Might girls be able to express anger when anger is the appropriate emotion instead of turning the negative feelings inward (which can then lead to depression)? Might boys be able to express sadness when sadness is the appropriate emotion instead of lashing out aggressively at a convenient target?

## Check Out Your Kids' Books for Stereotypes

One way to reduce stereotypes aimed at your children is to make sure the books in your house aren't stereotypical. Here are six quick ways to check your children's books for gender stereotypes.

1. Check the illustrations: Are all of the boys active and all of the girls passive? Are the girls sexualized?

2. Check the story line: Are the girls' problems always solved by a boy? Are the achievements of girls based on their own initiative and intelligence, or are they due to their good looks or relationships with boys? Are only boys portrayed as heroes? Are boys encouraged for being aggressive? Are boys ever shown as nurturing?

3. Note the friendships: Are boys and girls always separated? Are they ever portrayed as friends?

4. Consider the effect on your child's self-image: What happens to a girl's self-esteem when she reads that boys perform all of the brave and important jobs? What happens when all books depict only pretty and slim ("the fairest in the land") girls? What happens to a boy's self-esteem when he reads that all boys are supposed to be strong and bold?

5. Watch for loaded words: Are all animals "he"? Is the word "man" embedded in all the language ("chairman" instead of "chairperson," "fireman" instead of "firefighter")?

6. Look at the copyright date: Books published before 1973 are often sexist. There are, of course, many notable exceptions. But if the book is old, be sure to flip through it before giving it to your kids. If the book is worthwhile, but still has sexist themes, be sure to discuss them with your child.

—Based on recommendations from the Council on Interracial Books for Children

## Parenting at School

Parents also differ in how they subtly shape boys' and girls' academic pursuits. Parents routinely assume that their sons are more interested in math and science than their daughters. They also assume that math and science come more easily to their sons, whereas their daughters have to work harder for the same grades. Parents hold these assumptions regardless of how their kids are actually doing in math and science.[7] The alarming part is that their assumptions affect parents' actual behaviors.

Harriet Tenenbaum, a developmental psychologist now at the University of Surrey, along with Campbell Leaper at the University of California, Santa Cruz, visited families at their homes and asked them to participate in several science demonstrations. The researchers recorded how the parents and their children talked about the science demonstrations. During the physics task (which is most strongly associated with being a "boy subject"), fathers of sons used more cognitively demanding and interesting talk than did fathers of daughters (for example, by asking for causal explanations and using conceptual descriptions). Perhaps we shouldn't be surprised that boys become more interested in physics than girls, considering they are the ones having more interesting conversations about it.

Maybe sons are simply showing more interest in physics and their dads are matching their interest level? Tenenbaum would argue no. She also observed parents of preschoolers—brand new to science—at a science museum. Parents were three times more likely to explain the exhibits to sons than daughters. This is much more likely to be a parent-driven than a child-driven difference.[8]

Parents also shape boys' and girls' experiences with math. No one tells his or her daughter, "Girls are not good at math." But one thing parents do is intrude more on their daughters' math homework than their sons'.[9] They ask more often, "Are you sure about your answer?" and "Do you need help with that?" Understandably, their daughters feel less competent in math later on. Wouldn't you if someone was always trying to "help"? The girls begin to wonder whether they actually understand what they are doing in math.

There is a flip side for boys that can be just as harmful. If parents assume that boys understand math, and are less inclined to offer them help, the boy who struggles in math may go unnoticed. Again, these offers for help and intrusion into homework are not based on the child's actual performance. So parents may overestimate the math understanding of boys who struggle in math, while underestimating the math understanding of a girl who thrives in math. Neither situation is good for either kid.

These subtle assumptions about math also influence how we teach our kids in the early years. I stumbled upon this fact several years ago. When I was a professor of developmental psychology at UCLA, I worked next door to and became friends with Catherine Sandhofer, a developmental psychologist who studies how parents use language to teach their children concepts. She usually focuses on how preschoolers learn about words, shapes, and colors. She has no interest in studying gender stereotypes. Her graduate student, Alicia Chang, was working on a research study examining how parents talk to their preschoolers about numbers. They were analyzing a large public dataset that contains hundreds of hours of recorded conversations between parents and their children. These conversations were just the run of the mill conversations that occur at home and in cars between parents and their kids. Chang and Sandhofer wanted to know how parents talk informally with their young children in their everyday lives about numbers and quantities. This is important because it lays a crucial foundation for learning math later on.

I got involved because the data didn't turn out the way they expected. What they found was that the gender of the child swamped everything they originally thought was going to be important. Parents used numbers in talking to their toddler boys twice as much as when talking to toddler girls. So boys hear twice as much as girls that "You have two ears" or "Let's count the cars." When it came to talking about cardinal numbers (numbers that denote quantity), parents of boys mentioned numbers three times more often than parents of girls. So statements like, "You have five raisins left," were uttered to sons three times more often than to daughters.[10] I became involved because language researchers were forced to become gender researchers. As I told them, this research illustrates how we should not be surprised that middle-school boys end up being more comfortable than girls when talking about math, because clearly we have been grooming them for math from the beginning.

## THE GENDER POLICE

Parents operate as the de facto "gender police." Dads are the usual cops on the block, and sons are the most common targets. The area of a child's life that gets the most policing is in how they play. Parents are consistently more accepting of boys playing with boys' rather than girls' toys, and girls playing with girls' rather than boys' toys. Boys' play is the most strictly enforced. Indeed, fathers punish, criticize, or ridicule their sons for playing with girls' toys, even in laboratory studies where the boy was told to play with the toy.[11] Boys are usually blatantly discouraged from ever playing with dolls. Girls often have more flexibility with their parents, in that they are allowed (albeit not encouraged) to play with trucks. If you have sons, you likely know this rigid rule. Even if dad doesn't discourage his son from playing with dolls and kitchen sets, the adults in his life grimace or make side comments if a doll comes out.

These studies in which fathers criticize their sons for playing with dolls always remind me of the 1972 book and album *Free to Be . . . You and Me*, with the song "William Wants a Doll" (sung by Alan Alda and Marlo Thomas).[12] Maya is currently obsessed with playing this CD over and over. She loves the music, and I love the message. In the song, William wants a doll but everyone makes fun of him for it. William's dad tries to solve the problem by buying him "a basketball, a badminton set ... a baseball glove, and all the things a boy would love." Even though William loves sports, he continues to want a doll. His grandma buys him a doll and his father "began to frown." In 1972, the issue was gender stereotypes and fathers discouraging their sons from playing with dolls. Luckily, Grandma told everyone that William was just preparing to be a father himself one day. It seems like not much has changed since 1972.

Not all parents openly criticize their children for playing with cross-gender toys. Many parents just ignore cross-gender play and hope it will go away. Yvonne Caldera and her colleagues at the University of Kansas brought parent-toddler pairs into the lab. There were mothers with daughters, mothers with sons, fathers with daughters, and fathers with sons. They asked the parents to open a series of boxes and play with whatever toys were in them. Sometimes they were boy toys, like trucks and wooden blocks, and sometimes they were girl toys, like dolls and a kitchen set. Parents, especially dads, were noticeably more excited when they found a same-gender toy than a cross-gender toy. One dad of a daughter, upon opening a box with a truck in it, said, "Oh, they must have boys in this study." He promptly closed the truck box and went back to playing with the dolls from the previous box. He never even gave his daughter a chance to play with the truck. Eight parents actually had to be excluded from the analyses because they didn't even play with the cross-gender toys long enough to be analyzed.[13] It is like the opposite of *Field of Dreams*: If you ignore it, it will go away.

My impression of all the research on parenting boys and girls is that there aren't heavy-handed, explicit, noticeable differences. Parents, I am quite certain, would be horrified to think they treat their sons and daughters differently. They love their kids the same, hold the same overall goals for them, and use the same basic parenting approaches. But a parent's own comfort level—for example, while watching his or her son play with a baby doll—is going to register on the face with a grimace, wince, or look away. Even if parents bite their tongue when kids play with the "wrong" toy, kids notice these expressions.

Recall that from infancy, children look to their parent's face to know how to react. Psychologists call this social referencing. When your babies heard a loud noise, they would look to you to see whether they should be scared. When they saw something exciting, they would look to you to see whether you too were smiling. Kids pick up on these subtle reactions and use them to gauge their own reactions. They then change their behavior to elicit the most approval and positive attention. Remember, boys start out liking dolls just as much as girls do. The research clearly shows, however, that gender-police parents put a stop to that behavior pretty quickly.

## VARIETY IS THE SPICE OF LIFE

There are many reasons that I discourage parents from modifying their parenting based on the gender of their child. One reason is that it is simply more fun and fulfilling for parents when kids have a range of interests and skills rather than those dictated by stereotypes of boys or girls. If your daughter only likes Barbies, princesses, and dressing up, there is a limited range of activities you can do with her. It might be fun if a parent is interested in those activities too, but it won't be for others.

My husband, Kris, was dreading a life of Barbie Dream Houses when he realized he was going to have not one, but two daughters. I reminded him that doll play bores me, too. Dolls and dress-up were never my favorites as a child; I was much more interested in science experiments and art projects. I also reminded him that gender didn't have to determine everything our children did or played with. They are individuals, not just stereotypes of girls. And more importantly, they are our kids, part of our family. We can get them interested in the things we like to do. Kids can read your grimaces, but they can also read the joy on your face that comes from connecting with them over the activities that are meaningful to you.

Kris is a firefighter. His dad was a firefighter. His dad's dad was a firefighter. He works twenty-four-hour shifts, so when we want to visit him, we go to the fire station and the kids climb the fire engine. It seems only natural to me that Grace also loves firefighter play. We have two toy fire trucks that she can ride, a working water tank that can spray water, a firefighter suit and helmet, and countless tiny emergency vehicles. We even have two pairs of firefighter pajamas. Her favorite game is to ride around the house in her red plastic fire engine and put out pretend fires. She gets Maya involved in helping her "pump the water," screaming, "Pump, pump, pump!" Dad is always happy to help, sounding the alarm and turning the gas fireplace on so she can pretend to squirt water from her hose. I can see that he is having fun, reliving the same kind of games he played as a kid. I am glad he realized that kids are kids, if you raise them to just be kids.

There is no reason that girls should only like what Mom likes and boys should only like what Dad likes (okay, neither of my daughters think it is very exciting to be a professor; Kris has the market on occupational excitement). Part of the joy of parenting is exposing your children to your own passions and perspective on life. Why should that connection be limited to your same-gender children? Dads with daughters should have the same opportunities for connections, bonding, and mutual interests as dads with sons. And mothers should be able to bond with sons over shared activities just as they do with daughters.

It is ironic that dads are most often the gender police in families. Historically, fathers have been more removed from the day-to-day parenting tasks than mothers. This is definitely changing with the times, and I can quickly name dozens of dads who are changing that norm. But—particularly for more traditional dads, who might struggle with knowing exactly how to connect with their kids—wouldn't it be a lot easier if their children were invested in the activities that the dads also love? Even the dad who likes very male-typed activities, such as hunting, golf, architecture, or car shows, can instill a love of these things in both their boys and girls alike. The dad in the study I described above might have had a lot more fun playing with the truck in the new box instead of the dolls, but he stuck with the dolls because they were the "right" toy for his daughter. Sometimes, the gender of the child determines what we assume they will enjoy. What they will really enjoy is bonding with a parent over something they both love.

In other words, play with your kids the way you like to play! Take them to the exhibits, shows, or games that you would like to see. Talk to them about the topics that you are passionate about. Don't alter those experiences based on the gender of your child. And if you have both a son and a daughter, make sure both kids get the same exposure to you. Too many families pair up: moms with daughters and dads with sons. If you do this, your child's experiences are limited, halved, and your own emotional connection is also limited. Gender is a far less important detail about your child than the family he or she comes from. If all the major adults in a child's life ignored gender a little more, what an interesting, well-rounded, and emotionally connected child he or she could be.

## WHEN THE INDIVIDUAL
## DOESN'T FIT THE STEREOTYPE

Another reason that I encourage parents to focus on the individual instead of a stereotyped version of their kid is because most children don't fit the stereotypes. When we stop paying so much attention to gender alone, we can help our children face their own unique challenges and obstacles.

Raising a unique individual who doesn't always match the expected stereotype can sometimes have very important consequences. A conflict really came to a head in a middle school in Kentucky that decided to teach boys and girls in single-sex classrooms based on supposed "brain differences." In that school, the teachers taught boys in a highly competitive environment, because boys are supposed to be highly active, aggressive, and competitive. Boys were made to stand up during class, throw balls at one another as they answered questions, and take tests that were timed (to increase the excitement of the classroom).

The problem is that not all boys thrive in a highly active, competitive, and aggressive setting, because not all boys are highly active, competitive, and aggressive. There is a bell curve of activity, with some boys having a high activity level, others having a low activity level, and most being in the middle. Some boys are highly stressed and anxious when a ball is being heaved at their head during math. School became so stressful for some of those boys in their *Lord of the Flies* classrooms that their parents fought (unsuccessfully) to change the classrooms back to integrated ones. Their sons tried to live up to the stereotype. They tried to throw the ball and answer math questions. But they weren't stereotypes. Instead, they started falling behind in school, and their love of school turned into anxiety-filled mornings. Their parents learned the hard way that stereotypes about how a boy should learn didn't apply to their boys, because their boys are unique individuals and not stereotypes.

Often, parents—particularly parents of boys—desperately want their boys to be "just one of the guys." There is so much concern when boys show "too many" feminine traits or want to play with girl toys. The why is a little unclear. Some feminists (a label I apply to myself) argue that it is because anything feminine gets devalued in our culture. There is a lot of truth to that. Just look at the pay disparities between men and women. But, I think the answer here is simpler than that. I believe parents see a boy playing with a doll and think he will be gay, with the flawed conclusion that if he's stopped from playing with girl toys, he won't be gay. I hate to break it to you: playing with dolls doesn't make a boy gay. And preventing him from playing with dolls doesn't make him straight. Scientists aren't exactly sure how the complicated biological, neurological, and social factors combine to determine our sexuality, but Barbie ain't in the mix. Rather, parents who pressure their children into being more stereotypical than they naturally are often end up with children who are depressed and anxious. In other words, kids will either be gay or not, just like they will either have brown hair or not. It can't be encouraged or discouraged, simply accepted.

# When Children Want to Be the Other Gender

What happens when children want to be the other gender? Some children as young as two are diagnosed with gender identity disorder or, as it is now called, gender dysphoria. This is a controversial topic. Although it is rare (occurring in less than 1 percent of the population) some children reject the gender they are born with and all the trappings (clothes, traits, and activities) of that gender. In addition to wanting to be the other gender, a child may reject stereotypical play, toys, clothing, and activities, and may hate his or her own genitalia and want it to disappear. Children may hate their own gender so much that they become depressed. Gender dysphoria happens more often in boys (who want to be girls) than in girls (who want to be boys).

Parents are often deeply worried when their children show a strong desire to be the other gender. Oftentimes, parents' worry is less about children's accompanying depression but more about not wanting their child to be gay. The link, however, between gender dysphoria and sexual orientation is not clear. Some children who hate their gender do grow up to be homosexual. But plenty of homosexual adults were quite gender-stereotypical as children. And many children who show gender dysphoria as children "grow out of it" later.

What can parents do if their child seems to reject his or her gender? First, immediately help any child who is struggling with depression or anxiety. Any changes in behavior, appetite, attitudes about or performance in school, or mood should get a parent's attention. Depression warrants a visit to a pediatrician, a psychologist, or a social worker. Second, help him or her recognize the difference between biology and stereotypes. These kids should know that, regardless of their biological gender, they can dress how they want, play with what they want, and be friends with whomever they want. This is probably why this "disorder" is diagnosed more often in boys than girls. Girls are allowed to show masculine traits more freely than boys are to show feminine traits. Parents should accept all the variations that children come in. If children feel accepted by their parents and have the freedom to express themselves in ways that feel natural to them, they are much less likely to be depressed. That should be more important than fitting neatly into a box.

# START EARLY

The reality is that some children naturally fit the stereotype for their gender. Some girls are quiet, passive, nurturing, and sensitive. Some boys are high energy, loud, aggressive, and physical. For those kids, life will be a bit easier because the world is pretty tailored to them. For everyone else (and everyone else is much more common), they'll have traits that are stereotypical and traits that aren't. Maya loves her pink bedroom and sparkly headband. She also loves math, building with tools, and going to boat shows with her dad. She is great that way. Most kids are like that; they don't fit neatly into a box. My nephew is an excellent example of a boy who is sensitive and loves to read and draw but also loves Legos and Nerf guns—a really cool individual.

Here's a tip for parents: focus less on the stereotypes of girls and boys early on, wait a while to see what unique characteristics emerge, and then foster children's unique qualities. So that means bringing a baby home to a neutral-colored room (I personally love a happy grass-green paint) and lots of trucks and trains, stuffed animals, and dolls right from the start. Include plenty of up-close talking, snuggling, smiling, rough-and-tumble playing, reading, talking about numbers, and explaining science exhibits. Check the stereotypes and assumptions at the nursery door. This way kids turn out to just be kids: They will love some of the stuff you love. And they will have a range of traits that are unique to them and not neatly placed into a limiting pink or blue box.

# THE FINAL FOUR:
# WHAT ARE THE KEY ISSUES?

- Whether we mean to or not, many of us treat our sons and daughters differently. It is usually in subtle ways, like how often we talk about numbers or which chores we assign to each kid.

- Many parents encourage children to play with same-gender toys and discourage or ignore children playing with cross-gender toys. This subtle policing directs children to play with only the most stereotypical toys available.

- It is much more fulfilling for parents to engage their children in a range of activities, not just the ones stereotypically linked to that child's gender. Fathers of daughters shouldn't feel limited to a world of Barbie Dream Houses and mothers of sons shouldn't feel limited to a world of Little League.

- Parenting a stereotyped version of your child may work for some children, but not for most of them. Most children fit their gender stereotypes in some ways and not in others. Parenting should reflect that complicated uniqueness.

# Accidentally Shaping Who Children Become

**If someone asked me to name the** most difficult part of raising kids without gender stereotypes, my first answer would be the kids themselves. As I have discussed, kids latch on to our every use of "boys" and "girls." They tend to think in stereotyped terms and have a strong need for conforming to their group, which means they are major creators and enforcers of their own rigid (and often illogical) gender rules. But there is another tricky part to raising kids without stereotypes, and it is actually harder to fix than the first because it comes from parents themselves and is unintentional.

As described, we have our own stereotypes that influence our behavior, even when we don't really believe the stereotypes. We were, after all, raised and shaped in a stereotyped culture and we are not immune from the pressures of gender norms. Our own stereotypes may be subtle —but even when they are unstated and unintended, they can trickle down to our kids, who are detectives at reading our body language and unspoken thoughts. In this chapter, I describe how those unspoken, unintended stereotypes and expectations can shape our kids in ways that confirm and reinforce those very stereotypes. I then describe the emotional toll these stereotypes take on our kids, and how we can try to minimize our own (accidental) use of stereotypes.

## PYGMALION IN THE CLASSROOM

In 1963, Lenore Jacobson was a San Francisco elementary school principal when she read an article in the *American Scientist* written by Robert Rosenthal, a social psychologist at Harvard. Rosenthal was an emerging expert on how a researcher's expectations could influence the outcome of a study. He became interested in this issue after he had nearly ruined his own dissertation. He realized—too late—that he had unwittingly treated his experimental participants in such a way that led them to behave in accordance with his predictions. It had been unintentional. He learned the hard way that his own expectations about how the experiment should work must have elicited the very behaviors he expected.

After that experience, he began urging researchers to be "blind" to which participants were in which conditions, so that their own expectations couldn't influence the results (this is now a required part of research studies). In his article "On the Social Psychology of the Psychological Experiment," he tentatively suggested that teachers in the classroom might also be eliciting expected behaviors from their students.[1] When Lenore Jacobson read this, she was immediately interested and wrote to Rosenthal and a correspondence began between the two. She offered her assistance to Rosenthal and a study idea was born. A year later, he traveled to San Francisco to visit her and they hashed out the details. The results of this collaboration were published in a 1968 book called *Pygmalion in the Classroom* (and have since been replicated many times).[2]

Using Jacobson's school, they gave all the children an IQ test at the beginning of the school year. They kept the real test results secret from the teachers. They told the teachers the children had just taken the

"Harvard Test of Inflected Aptitude," something that sounds impressive but was totally made up. Rosenthal and Jacobson told the teachers that 20 percent of the students performed so well on the test that they would show remarkable gains in intellectual competence over the school year. They were referred to as "bloomers." Those 20 percent of students didn't actually score any better than anyone else; they were selected entirely at random.

So the teachers went ahead with their school year teaching the kids as they normally would. Rosenthal and Jacobson came back and measured the children's IQs again after eight months with their teachers, the same teachers who believed that some of their students were especially likely to succeed. What did they find? Among the first and second graders, the "bloomers" had increased their IQ scores by more than twice the increases other children experienced. By the end of the school year, the teachers described these children as smart, interesting, likeable, affectionate, and more likely to succeed than the others. Remember, these children started out no different from anyone else. But the teachers believed that they were likely to improve the most. Without meaning to, the teachers elicited the exact behavior they expected.

## PYGMALION AT HOME

This effect, drawing out the very behaviors you expect, is not restricted to the classroom. Parents do this, too. It's fine when expectations are unbiased, but they usually differ by gender. Returning to math as an example, studies have repeatedly shown that parents think math is more natural for boys than girls. If a girl excels in math, parents often assume that it's simply because of hard work, not because of innate abilities. Mothers of girls typically underestimate their daughters' mathematical abilities; mothers of boys overestimate their sons' abilities. When parents have low expectations, over time, their daughters become less confident about their math abilities, begin to think that math isn't very useful, and take fewer high school math classes. You might assume that parents are just tuned in to kids' actual abilities, but that isn't the case. Parents' beliefs and expectations are better predictors of children's own beliefs than actual grades. In other words, my daughter's own beliefs about how good she is at math are more based on my beliefs about her competence than on any grade she might actually get in math. That is a lot of parental power.

Kids begin to behave and perform in line with parental expectations. When parents have high expectations, children often strive to live up to them, working harder, believing they can succeed at the task as well as improve and excel. On the flip side, when parents have lower expectations, children assume the task is difficult, believe they can't really achieve much, and thus don't try quite as hard. This is a recipe for low performance, confirming the very expectations that started the domino effect.

Oftentimes, our expectations for our children are driven by our own internalized gender stereotypes that we are not even aware of, stereotypes that are deep-seated, rooted there from your childhood, and impervious to the many contradictory examples you have seen over your life. For example, I grew up totally buying into the idea that girls aren't good at math. I don't believe the stereotype, but I was definitely shaped by it. I would still say I am not strong at math, despite having a PhD minor in statistics. So even though I don't believe the stereotype, and have evidence to disprove the stereotype, it is still stuck in the back of my head. When Maya was little, I never expected her to excel in math. I just assumed that I didn't love math, so she probably wouldn't love it.

Because of my concerns about passing along gender stereotypes, she and I talked a lot about math when she was a preschooler. We did basic addition (like counting how many raisins she would have if I gave her my raisins) and talked about numbers. She also went to a Montessori preschool that did an excellent job of making math a concrete and fun activity. For whatever reason, she happens to love math now and is quite talented at it, so my expectations have since shifted. But I had to make a conscious effort to recognize my own biases and change them. As we see time and again, once something is stuck in our head, it will come out in our behavior and is really hard to stop unless we make a concerted effort and pay attention.

How exactly do our own unintended stereotypes and expectations influence our kids? I will first describe the subtle ways that our deep-seated attitudes shape our kids through nonverbal cues, and then how our attitudes can accidently shape our more explicit parenting behaviors.

## WHEN OUR STEREOTYPES SHOW

Stereotypes come out in ways that are extremely subtle and almost impossible to control. Kind of like the carbon monoxide of attitudes, seeping into your house, odorless and colorless, poisoning everyone without your knowledge. Psychologists refer to them as implicit attitudes, to contrast them with the explicit attitudes that are much easier to detect and change. We all hold them—even feminist psychologists who write books about gender stereotypes (ahem, me).

### Reflection

Imagine a high school physics class. The top student has earned an A in the class and is preparing to take the AP Physics exam. This student, who also earned an A in trigonometry, has been eagerly following the internationally famous discovery of the Higgs Boson particle and is considering an internship with an astrophysicist. The physics teacher writes the student a stellar letter of recommendation for college scholarships.

Now retell this story. Describe what this student looks like. In your retelling, which pronoun did you use: he or she (notice I never mentioned the gender of the student)? I know that my own mental image was of a boy, not a girl.

The unintended stereotypes we hold in our brains get stuck in there because we live immersed in a culture soaked in stereotypes. Sheer exposure to media shapes us, especially because we only see movies and TV shows with male scientists and female teachers, and where men are either fighting or philandering and women are either cleaning or crying. You see something enough times, and your brain makes the connections; you cannot stop it. Importantly, your brain holds on to these implicit, hidden stereotypes even when you disagree with them. You can say, and truly believe, that men and women are just the same, but your brain holds on to stereotypes like a toddler with her tattered but beloved blankie.

These hidden, unintended stereotypes are usually conveyed with nonverbal cues in your body language. This isn't a lot different than a "tell" in poker, which are the nonverbal cues that indicate whether you have a good or bad hand. In the James Bond movie *Casino Royale*, Bond realizes his archenemy twitches his eye whenever he is bluffing. People don't mean to give these clues away; they are simply hard to control. It is the same with stereotypes. When children are behaving stereotypically, we smile and nod frequently and make more eye contact. We lean in, and our body posture is relaxed. Kids, channeling their inner James Bond, detect these changes in body language. Kids can even detect these nonverbal cues in strangers in a video clip, and they use those cues to form their own stereotypes.[3] Body language that conveys approval leads children to do more of the approved behavior. What would your body language be like if your son were playing with a Barbie? You would likely stiffen up and maybe look away. He would notice these subtle changes and adapt accordingly.

You may question whether kids can really pick up on these subtle nonverbal cues. They can and do. Even a horse can do it. The story of Clever Hans is famous in psychology history books. Clever Hans was a horse in the early 1900s who supposedly could solve math problems. His owner would ask him, "What is 100 divided by 4?" and the horse would tap twenty-five times with his hoof. He was quite the spectacle, traveling throughout Germany amazing fans, answering any math question posed to him.

Because there was such public interest in Clever Hans, an investigation was launched into the scientific claims that a horse really had arithmetic abilities. The investigation discovered that the owner was involuntarily giving nonverbal cues to Hans when he was approaching the right answer. The owner would smile and lean closer as Hans tapped the numbers, and Clever Hans, being clever, read these cues and gauged his answers appropriately. Even the investigator, whose goal had been to rebuke any claims about Hans, couldn't help but give Hans the same involuntary cues when he himself was questioning the horse. The only time Hans missed math problems was when the questioner didn't know the answer or the horse had on blinders.[4] In other words, even a horse (albeit a clever one) can pick up on subtle, involuntary body language. It isn't surprising, therefore, that kids can.

## FROM PARENTS' BELIEFS TO KIDS' BEHAVIOR

Sometimes parents' subtle stereotypes and beliefs can also shape their children's behavior in more obvious, yet still unintended, ways. Stereotypes can come out in more explicit parenting behaviors. In 1987, Jacquelynne Eccles, a psychology professor at the University of Michigan, and her colleagues began a research project called "Childhood and Beyond." This study followed almost one thousand children and their families from first through twelfth grade (and into adulthood). They wanted to know what leads some teenagers to choose certain activities versus other activities. Over time, they became particularly interested in why girls were pulling away from math and sciences in high school. They found a direct line of influence from parents to their children: parents' beliefs influenced their behaviors, and their behaviors influenced their children's motivation and later behaviors.[5]

Let's break down that process into what it really means: Parents hold certain beliefs about their children's abilities. How would you answer if, like the parents in the study, you were asked, "How good is your child at math?" What would you say about reading, music, and sports? How would you answer if you were asked, "Compared with other children, how much innate ability or talent does your child have in math?" What would you say about reading, music, and sports? How would you respond to "How important is it to you that your child does well in math?" and the more personal, and hard to change, "How confident do you feel about your own ability to help in math?" Unfortunately, parents' attitudes reflected the gender stereotypes you might expect. Girls are thought to be better at reading and music, and boys are thought to be better at math and sports.

These attitudes, about how good their child is at something and how important the activities are, guide parents' behaviors. First, parents who believe their children are good at some type of activity, and who think it is important for their children to do well at that activity, are more likely to model those activities. This is sometimes purposeful, but oftentimes it isn't. You model reading when you sit on the couch and read a novel for fun. You model athletics when you jog or ride your bike on a sunny Saturday afternoon. You model math when you play a math game. You model music when you play an instrument or turn on the radio.

Second, parents who think their children excel at something and believe it is important are also more likely to provide activity-related materials, such as math games, books, musical instruments, or athletic equipment. Take an inventory of your own life. Does your child see you read for pleasure, jog, or play Sudoku? Does your child have balls, books, math games, and puzzles around the house? Parents provide materials for activities they think are important. Stereotypically, in this study I have been describing, boys were provided with far more equipment for sports than girls were. Does your daughter have plenty of balls, a bike, jump ropes, and rackets? Does she have math games or workbooks? Does your son have plenty of books and opportunities to paint or play music?

Third, parents who think their children excel at something and believe it is important are more likely to explicitly encourage their kids and are more likely to participate in the activity with their kids. As expected, boys were encouraged more in math and sports, and girls were encouraged more in music and reading. Think about your own life again. Did you play sports with your child this week, take him or her to a concert, read to your child or vice versa, or solve math problems together? I find myself guilty of being stereotypical in some ways and not in others. As I mentioned, Maya loves math and frequently wants me to give her algebra problems to solve. So we sit together, and I make up an equation to solve for x, and she does it on her handheld dry erase board. But when she wants to hit a softball outside, I do it for about five minutes. I believe her math, music, and reading abilities are stronger than her athletic abilities, and as predicted by the researchers, I spend more time working with her on those activities. Even as I write this, I am struck by the irony. I spend more time with her doing the things she already excels at. I should probably spend more time on her weakest skills, but like most parents, I focus my time and attention on the perceived strengths.

The researchers found that parents (and teachers alike) indeed differ on how they encourage stereotypical behaviors. Parents are more engaged when their child's behavior is stereotypical. They lean in closer, offer more interaction, and share more information about the topic. They ask more difficult questions and give kids more opportunities to get the right answer. They offer more explicit encouragement and more critical feedback.

And here is where the process gets really important. Parents' behaviors influence what their children think about their own abilities:

- Parents who are more encouraging and engaged in an activity because they believe their child has more ability in that activity, have children who become, in fact, better at the activity and enjoy the activity more—independent of the child's actual abilities.

- These parents, in turn, encourage those activities more, model them more often, and provide more activity-related materials. This further fosters the child's improvment at the skill. Practice does make perfect after all.

- It's logical that the children begin to like the activity even more than before and perceive themselves to be good at it.

Why does that matter? When kids enjoy something and feel good at it, they are more likely to continue doing it and will continue to improve. For example, a child who is encouraged to read will begin to enjoy reading more and view themselves as good at reading, which means they will read more frequently. Reading more frequently is the best way to improve at reading. This really matters, for example, in contexts like signing up for high school math classes: kids who felt more competent in math, largely predicted by mom's beliefs early on, were more likely to be taking advanced math classes in high school.

## PRAISE IS A FUNNY THING

It is important not to confuse encouragement with praise. Children don't want easy praise; they want to earn it. It is important not to toss praise around lightly. Easy praise is "Great job! You are doing so well." Encouragement is "You are working really hard! I know you can figure out these problems. Keep at it! I am proud of you." It is a subtle, but really important distinction. Praise, when the task is easy, tells kids that you have low expectations for them. This actually leads kids to feel less competent. If I praised Maya for solving basic addition problems ("What is 4 plus 6?" "10? Great job!"), she would roll her eyes at me. When kids hear a teacher praise another child for something easy, they rate the other child as having low abilities in that task. When children are offered unneeded help, they feel incompetent and report feeling anger, worry, disappointment, distress, and anxiety. They also feel less confidence, less pride in their accomplishments, and less satisfaction. (I am sometimes overwhelmed by how tough it is to raise kids! You try to praise them to boost them up and all you do is make them feel bad about themselves.)

Instead, tell your children that you have high expectations for them. Then, offer constructive feedback if they have poor performance. Offering constructive feedback (which is not the same as criticism) shows that you have high expectations and that you think your child has the ability to meet those expectations. For example, if your son is writing an essay for homework and it isn't very good, instead of assuming he can't do better, tell him that he can do better. Offer specific places where he could improve, such as "Why don't you start with a topic sentence?" or "Perhaps you can describe this part in a little more detail." Constructive feedback is specific and focused on how to improve, and it is the kind of encouragement that helps kids both believe in their own abilities and improve, which, in turn, helps children stick with activities they might otherwise have struggled with.

This is also how we fight our own internal stereotypes. If your child is in elementary school, don't praise your daughter for simple math or athletic feats or your son for reading an easy passage or writing a basic sentence. Offer encouragement and constructive feedback. Assume they can excel at all of those tasks, even if you didn't.

## THE IMPACT OF SUBTLE EXPECTATIONS

All of these subtle pressures directed at kids—the approving head nods, the extra boost of encouragement, the book you bought that wasn't really necessary but looked interesting—shape kids over time in meaningful ways. It doesn't take grand statements by you, teachers, or the media; gentle nudges in one direction instead of another direction make the most impact.

My family is from the rural South and I spent a lot of my childhood standing beside creek beds looking for smooth shiny pebbles, as those were the best for skipping across the water. I was always amazed at the power of rushing water that could, given enough time, smooth away the rough edges of any given rock. Even gentle creeks have smoothing powers with enough time and pressure. Kids are like river rocks and childhood is full of time and pressure.

The power of parenting is in the little moments, usually in the moments we don't mean to be "parenting." In my opinion, this is what makes parenting so hard. It would be easy if kids eagerly approached you on your best days, the days you felt rested and relaxed, saying, "Mom, Dad, teach me something important so I can live a happy and productive life." They would soak up your pearls of wisdom then and ignore all the times you were overwhelmed, snapped at family members for no reason, yelled at the driver who cut you off on the highway, or commented about feeling fat in your jeans in front of your teenage daughter.

It would be much easier if kids only paid attention when you wore your "parenting hat" and not when your own worse traits popped up. This is never so obvious as when you see your kids reflecting back your worse traits (such as swear words and mannerisms). It was funny when Grace yelled at Maya, "You've gotta be kidding me!" (something I apparently utter), but not so funny when I see Maya cry over minor frustrations (something I also do). They pay attention to it all—the good and the bad, the intentional and the accidental.

When we are stressed out, what psychologists call being under cognitive load, our unintended, implicit stereotypes are most likely to seep out. It probably isn't too difficult to imagine being stressed out because you are simultaneously cooking dinner, supervising homework, calling the plumber about the clogged drain, and responding to an email from a disgruntled coworker. This is exactly when you are least able to challenge stereotypes. So when your daughter is working on math homework or your son complains about a bully at school, your own hidden stereotypes are most likely to influence your reaction. You may be dismissive of your son's concerns or roll your eyes at his expressed sadness, or blindly praise your daughter for easy work or be overly intrusive in the work she already knows how to do. Since it's not possible to rid ourselves of all the stressful moments in our lives, and our children are going to continue to be shaped by these moments we least expect, the best way to shape our kids is to change ourselves.

## THE EMOTIONAL TOLL OF STEREOTYPES

Gender stereotypes take an emotional toll on children. Being shaped into something that is culture-specific (which is what gender stereotypes are), rather than something true to the individual, is never easy.

Here are some examples. Boys who think that parenting is a job mothers do best (with all of their "mother's intuition") grow up to be men who make the same assumption. Those men tend to leave much of the "mothering" behavior to their wives. They aren't the dads doing the middle-of-the-night feedings and skinned-knee kissing. They assume that moms are there for the warm and fuzzy stuff, as their moms were the ones who gave them knee kisses as young boys. The result of this gender stereotype is that those fathers miss out on many of the joys of parenting. Granted, they may be more well rested, but their babies are not as securely attached to them as the fathers who wade into the 2:00 a.m. trenches. This means their toddlers are less likely to run to them when they need a comforting hug and less likely to call out for them after the nightmare in the middle of the night.[6]

Importantly, the dads who avoid the "mom" stuff end up less satisfied with parenting than other dads. The studies showing this don't surprise me. I know how it feels when my kids are sad or scared and a hug from me puts their world right again. Those soul-soaring moments, when you know you truly met your children's emotional needs, make every sleep-deprived, dirty-diapered, snotty-nosed moment worth it. These dads love their kids, and their kids love them; it just isn't as fulfilling a role in life as it could have been had these fathers ditched the stereotype. This is why I talk so much about boys playing with dolls (and why your body language and comments shouldn't show disapproval when they do). Knowing how to caretake and nurture helps boys become the kind of fathers who can find deep joy in parenting.

Another example of the emotional toll focuses on girls. Girls have their own set of stereotypes to live up to. One particularly damaging one that packs an emotional wallop is the stereotype that girls should be pretty and thin. Girls who believe in gender stereotypes, especially the ones that say girls should always be pretty, are more likely to suffer depression by the time they enter middle school.[7] It is a hard ideal to live up to in real life, especially as girls enter adolescence and those fun "awkward" years.

Also, the more girls believe in these "girls should be thin and pretty" stereotypes, the more negative is their body image.[8] In other words, a girl who believes in gender stereotypes is more likely to think her own body is far different from what she would like her body to be and what she thinks other girls want their bodies to be. This is why half of adolescent girls in the U.S. are on some form of a diet, starting as young as age eight.[9] These stereotypes are why I enforce a no-Barbie/no-Bratz house. My kids have plenty of dolls that have realistic bodies. Girls have a more negative body image after playing with Barbie than before.[10] Who needs those stereotypes about what a woman should look like sneaking in during playtime?

Girls who buy into this ideal that they should be pretty and thin also don't realize that pretty can go hand-in-hand with smart. Lee Anne Bell, an education professor now at Barnard College at Columbia University, interviewed gifted third- through sixth-grade girls. In their interviews, the girls talked about downplaying their intelligence because they wanted to appear pretty. They also didn't want to look like they were bragging or being competitive.[11] Their stereotyped ideal was to look pretty, act pretty, and not be too smart—a tough road.

There is an important distinction to note: Those emotional knocks don't affect African-American girls as much as they do white girls. As a group, African-American girls have better self-esteem, less depression, and better body image, and feel more in control. One of the most important reasons why this is so is because of their mothers. In studies, African-American girls have more positive relationships with their mothers than do white girls. African-American mothers more strongly encourage their independence (something white moms more often save for sons). Having moms foster their independence helped the girls feel better and more confident about themselves.[12]

## CHECKING STEREOTYPES
## AT THE NURSERY DOOR

So what are parents to do? As a first step, be aware of your own stereotypes:

- Do your attitudes about your children's abilities and interests reflect their true performance? How do you know?

- Did you begin having certain expectations as soon as you saw the sonogram?

- Try to reevaluate your own ideas about what boys are like, what girls are like, and what the innate differences are between the two.

The second step is to decide which skills and abilities are important to you. Let me help:

- Math, science, and reading help your child do well throughout school.

- Physical activity helps your child live a healthy life.

- Nurturance, empathy, and taking the perspective of others help your child have meaningful relationships throughout life.

Notice that gender should never be relevant to any of these skills and abilities.

The rest of the list is up to you. Now that you know what you want to instill, are you modeling these behaviors yourself? Are you encouraging them in your kids? Are you providing materials for your children to use that foster these skills? Are you giving them opportunities to pursue them?

The third step is to continue to check yourself whenever your child is doing something stereotypical or nonstereotypical:

- Do you show more approval when your daughter plays dolls or acts like a princess than when she plays with cars?

- Do you show more approval when your son plays rough outside than when he plays with dolls?

These are subtle signs of approval, like a smile or a nod. Just be conscious of your own nonverbal cues and how your child's behavior confirms or disconfirms your own expectations.

## THE FINAL FOUR: WHAT ARE THE KEY ISSUES?

- As parents, our own expectations can elicit the very behavior we expect in our kids. Those expectations often differ by gender.

- Our kids can detect our nonverbal cues of approval or disapproval and shape their behaviors accordingly. Kids know what an approving smile means, and they like it much better than a disapproving frown.

- Parents who assume their kids excel at something set their kids up to excel even more, by encouraging them, modeling the skill for them, and providing more opportunities to practice the skill. So if you assume your son or daughter is good at something, odds are you will accidentally make him or her good at it.

- We have to change our own deep-seated, hidden stereotypes. We all have them, so all we can do is make sure they don't seep out into our parenting. Otherwise, the emotional toll on our kids can be a whopper.

## CHAPTER 10

# Stereotype Sneak Attacks

**Imagine you have done everything** I have argued for in this book. You reduced your use of gender in your everyday language and parenting decisions. You've stocked a wide variety of toys in your house from birth. You don't assume your daughter will like something just because she is a girl. You don't assign your son certain chores just because he is a boy. You invite both boys and girls over to play and to your kids' birthday parties. You correct your kids when you hear them state a stereotype. You encouraged your high school daughter to take AP Calculus and reiterated that you expected her to do well in the class (after all, you did spend much of her toddler years talking to her about numbers and basic math).

She takes the class and does well in it, earning an A. First of all, congratulations! You've already accomplished a lot by having your daughter take an advanced math class, a task many girls shy away from. Now, she signs up to take the standardized AP Calculus test to earn AP credit for college (which means there is one less class she will have to take in college). She sits down in the testing classroom, surrounded by more boys than girls. The male teacher passes out the exams to everyone and writes the time on the board. Even though you have explicitly taught her that girls are just as good at math as boys, she knows the stereotype about girls and math. She doesn't believe it, but she knows it (because, thankfully, you didn't raise her in a cave). The AP test is in the standard format, one in which kids indicate their name, grade, school, ethnicity, and gender on the cover page before starting the math problems. And so begins the sneakiest of stereotype effects.

By circling "girl" on the front page, her brain had to think about her gender for a split second. This unintentionally activated the stereotype about girls doing poorly in math, even though it is a stereotype she doesn't believe and that she herself proves false. Because of reasons I will discuss in a minute, by thinking about her gender before the test, she actually does worse on the test than she could have. It wasn't a lot worse, but it was just enough to not get that AP credit (students have to score a certain percentage correct on the test to earn AP credit). Analyses of national AP Calculus tests shows that almost five thousand additional girls a year would have scored high enough to earn AP credit had they indicated their gender at the end of the test instead of the beginning.[1] Simply pushing back those gender thoughts until the test is over can keep performance higher.

This effect is called stereotype threat and it illustrates how, even when we don't pass gender stereotypes along to our kids, the mere existence of stereotypes out in the world affects them. In this chapter, I'll discuss what stereotype threat is, how stereotypes can impact children even when your child doesn't believe them, and how you can help protect your kids from these negative effects.

## WHAT IS STEREOTYPE THREAT?

Whenever a negative stereotype about a group exists, the people in that group are worried about living up to that negative stereotype. They don't want to confirm anyone's less-than-flattering preconceived notions about them. This is true of any group you can imagine. We all have negative stereotypes associated with our groups. It can be girls in math, boys at reading, or sixty-year-old white men at dunking a basketball. It can be kids from poor families on IQ tests or elderly folks on a memory task. It can be white men in math, if they are being compared to Asian men in math. It can be straight A college students, if they attend a public state university and are compared to Ivy League students. It can even be high-achieving female math majors at an Ivy League university, if being compared to male math majors.

We have all experienced a moment of stereotype threat. The details are always different, but the feeling is the same. You walk into a room or approach a situation and think, "Oh, crap! I am the only [fill in your label: man/Latino/Southerner/parent/forty-year-old] here. I really hope I don't suck at this and embarrass myself." My most recent personal example of stereotype threat involved being a panelist on a symposium called "What's New in Science?" It was me (a psychologist), with a chemist, a physicist, and a geologist. I was definitely aware of being the only "soft" scientist. Our job was to listen to the other panelists give research presentations and ask follow-up questions. I remember thinking to myself, "I hope I don't ask a stupid question."

My husband describes the time when he took our then infant Grace out in public and needed to change her diaper. He said he felt all the moms in the room peer at him as he changed the diaper, seemingly checking to see if he was doing it right. Whether they were or weren't isn't the point. He felt that he had something to prove about being a competent dad, just like I felt I needed to prove my "science chops" on the panel. Neither of us believes those negative stereotypes (that men can't be qualified parents or that psychologists can't handle hard science), but we definitely didn't want our own performances to feed into those stereotypes for others. That moment of concern, even when it is a split second, is when a stereotype is a threat. Why? Because that momentary worry can actually make my science question seem stuttering and can make Kris clumsily change a diaper, despite deftly handling these tasks many times before.

Claude Steele, a professor of psychology at Stanford University, along with fellow researcher Joshua Aronson, first coined the term *stereotype threat* in 1995 as a way of describing those situations when we are at risk of confirming a negative stereotype about our group. It is an ironic process. We are at risk of confirming the negative stereotype because of our concern about confirming the stereotypes.[2] Since 1995, hundreds of studies have confirmed this: people are worried (usually subconsciously) about living up to negative stereotypes. This worry can interfere with their ability to do well on the very thing they were concerned about. So any situation that triggers even subconscious thoughts of a stereotype can actually lower a person's performance in that situation, which unfortunately serves to confirm the very stereotype he or she was worried about. There's no point mincing words: stereotypes are a real pain in the ass.

## Learning More about Stereotype Threat

Stereotype threat is a very specific topic of research within psychology and education. Hundreds of studies have been conducted on the topic within the past twenty years, and most of them are pretty straightforward and appropriate for a nonacademic.

If you are interested in learning more, I recommend reading Dr. Claude Steele's *Whistling Vivaldi: How Stereotypes Affect Us*. Steele is the preeminent researcher on this phenomenon, and he's also a great writer. He starts his book on a personal note, describing his experiences as a black child in Chicago during segregation.[3]

I also recommend www.reducingstereotypethreat.org. It was created by researchers and does an excellent job of compiling all of the latest research on stereotype threat in one place for the public.

# HOW DOES STEREOTYPE THREAT WORK?

The worst part of stereotype threat is that it affects the people who care most about their performance, such as students who want to be good at school. The more your child cares about being good at something, the more vulnerable he or she is to stereotype threat. This is because those people who care the most about being good are the ones most concerned with not conforming to some negative stereotype. Also, stereotype threat doesn't have to be something your child carries around every day. Your daughter may never think about being stigmatized in math, but one situation could trigger this concern and reduce her math performance—and she would never know it.

Let me break down exactly what happens. Stereotype threat can affect anyone given the right (or rather, wrong) situation. For example, stacks of research articles have been conducted on girls in math, leadership, or athletic tasks. But this affects boys too, particularly boys in elementary school who are "supposed" to be academically inferior to girls.[4]

## Step One: Knowing the Stereotype Exists

So imagine your eight-year-old son is sitting in his classroom about to take a standardized test (if you have only daughters, imagine the same story but with a girl in math or PE class). He knows that boys are supposed to be the troublemakers in school and get lower grades than girls. (As mentioned earlier in the book, kids know about these stereotypes by about age five, around the age they enter school. So right when academic performance begins to matter, knowledge of the stereotype starts to have an impact.) Your son also knows this stereotype isn't really true, but that a lot of people believe it.

## Step Two: Triggers

Something in the situation triggers your son to think about either his gender, the stereotype, or the test. This can happen in many different, and often mundane, ways:

1. He could be asked to circle his gender on the front page of the test.

2. His well-meaning teacher could ask him whether he has brothers or sisters (which oddly enough triggers thoughts of gender), or whether he likes sports (which triggers a boy stereotype).

3. His teacher could have been killing time prior to the start of the test and given him a coloring-book picture of a boy holding a baseball bat to color at his desk.

4. He could be the only boy in the testing room.

5. He could have a female teacher.

6. He could be told that the test is a measure of his academic abilities.

All of these scenarios have actually been used in research studies and are sufficient to trigger stereotype threat in the student.

The worst example I ever witnessed in a real classroom was a fourth-grade class I was observing (we were conducting a study about ethnic identity, so this was a surprise example). The teacher was teaching math by having the students answer questions at the chalkboard. His strategy: line the kids up girl-boy-girl-boy. So the teacher literally said, "Now, I need a girl." Then she had to go to the front of the class and answer a math problem in front of her classmates. Nothing subtle about triggering thoughts of gender here. As we see, this is perhaps the worst possible way to help her answer the math problem quickly and correctly.

## Step Three: Worries

The triggering of the negative stereotype leads your eight-year-old son to worry about confirming the stereotype. He doesn't want to be academically inferior to girls simply because he is a boy. Because he doesn't want to confirm the stereotype, he is likely to feel some anxiety. He may have an increase in cortisol (a stress hormone) and a general increase in physiological arousal. This minor worry is just enough to reduce his working memory. This means he may have a harder time reading a passage and answering comprehension questions on the test. His expectations for his performance may be lowered and he may be thinking more discouraging thoughts (such as "This test is really hard"). Importantly, though, he may be totally unaware of what is going on.

The best analogy for this process is a dirty boat. There is slime, algae, maybe even a barnacle or two on the bottom of the hull. These aren't major obstacles to the boat working properly. They are actually rather small. The boat can still speed along the lake. But that algae offers just enough water resistance to drag the boat down from its maximum speed. It reduces efficiency just enough to tack on some time and use more fuel. That is what the stereotype threat does. It is a drag on our efficiency and performance. The student may be completely unaware of what is going on, and the effects won't be drastic. But the effects are consistent and can translate into real performance deficits.

## Step Four: Impact on Performance

Because of the mental baggage of the previous step, there is some drag on how well your son can perform, and he doesn't do as well on his standardized test as he could have. It isn't that he forgot the material, doesn't care about the test, or slacks off because it is a "girl thing." No. He cares, he wants to do well, and he does okay—just not as well as he could have done in a different situation. Think about it. It is hard to perform your best if you have stress hormones pulsing through your body, you feel anxious, your working memory is tapped out, and you expect to do poorly. You are probably going to miss a couple of the trickier items, make a couple of careless errors (like putting the decimal point in the wrong place), or work more slowly. These are the types of things that happen simply because he had to indicate his gender before the test.

# AN IMPACT YOU CAN SEE

Stereotype threat can make your child do just a little worse on a big test if the situation makes him or her think about gender or the stereotype. This wouldn't be such a big deal if it only happened once. But, usually, it happens much more frequently. Over time, the negative effects start to add up and get worse. What are some of the impacts you can see over time?

There is, of course, decreased performance. This is the big one. It can happen in any situation where there is a negative stereotype. This can be at school if children are in a class that is stereotyped for the other gender. This can be at a game or a performance if it doesn't fit the "right" stereotype for their group. It can even be in a subject that they are supposed to excel at, as long as they are reminded that another group can do it better (such as white boys in math compared to Asian boys).

After doing worse than intended, kids may then blame themselves for the failure. This is referred to as an internal attribution. For example, a girl in a math class may mutter to herself after getting a lower grade than she wanted, "I am just not very good at math." But blaming yourself for a poor performance is no fun. No one likes to think they are stupid. We would rather blame something else. So the next effect of stereotype threat is a rise in self-handicapping. It is much better to blame a poor performance on a lack of studying or practice than low ability. And that is what people sometimes do. When stereotype threat is activated, individuals may practice less, study less, or claim to be under extra stress prior to taking the test. They handicap themselves before the stereotype can. To avoid blaming themselves, they give themselves an excuse for doing poorly. The rub is that by studying and practicing less, they actually set themselves up for future failure.

Another trick to avoid blaming themselves is to blame the test. Kids who just experienced stereotype threat may say that the test was tricky or unfair or not a good estimate of their ability. This is like saying, "I am good at math, but that test was just about geometry. That isn't even math. That is so unfair!" This can lower their motivation to take similar tests in the future. It is hard to get motivated to excel at something you think is unfair or unreasonable.

Over time, all of these coping strategies start to wear students down. Repeat low performances, trying to figure out something else to blame besides themselves, and the recurring bouts of anxiety over trying to do well begin to take a toll. So the final impact of stereotype threat is an act of pushing away from the table and saying, "I'm done." Students will disengage from the subject. Girls will start to say, "Who cares about math? I don't." And remember, they were only vulnerable to stereotype threat because they started out caring about math. A boy may say, "I don't care that I got a bad grade on this book report. At least I did well at my soccer game." They start to separate their own self-worth from their performance. This leads to eventually disidentifying with the domain entirely. Your daughter may avoid taking calculus because she says, "I am just not a math student." Children literally and permanently remove themselves from the threat situation—period, end of story. They completely separate their view of themselves from the stereotyped domain. Once that happens, it is really difficult to go back.

Stereotypes and the threat that accompanies them can even affect the types of careers our kids choose for themselves. Paul Davies, a professor of psychology at the University of British Columbia, conducted a really clever—yet disturbing—study about how easy it is to activate stereotype threat and how deep-reaching the effects can be. As part of his dissertation research, he recruited college girls at the University of Waterloo in their second semester of calculus. These young women all had a B or better in their class, and they all strongly believed they were good at math and felt that being good at math was extremely important.[5]

Davies showed these high-achieving young women a set of commercials—just regular commercials anyone might see on TV. Half of the girls saw stereotypical commercials. One commercial showed a woman so excited about her acne cream that she was bouncing for joy on her bed. The other depicted a woman drooling with desire over a new brownie mix. The other half of the girls saw neutral commercials—one about a cell phone and one about a pharmacy. That was all Davies did. He never mentioned that girls are bad at math. He never said, "I can't believe all you ladies have good grades in calculus. Go home and make your boyfriend a sandwich." He simply let them watch a bit of TV; no mention of gender, math, or academic stereotypes.

The girls then completed twelve items from the math portion of the GRE. It is challenging, no doubt, as it is used for admissions into graduate schools. But these are smart students. What happened? The girls who watched women get excited by acne cream and brownies solved fewer math items correctly than the girls who watched the ad about a cell phone. They were all making good grades in college calculus and loved math, but the stupid (and I mean that literally) stereotype came in and tripped them up. Not only did they do worse on the math questions, but when given the chance to do some extra questions from the math and verbal sections of the GRE, they tried fewer math questions and tried more verbal questions. That simple activation of the stereotype, watching an everyday commercial, led good math students to pull away from math and into a proper "girl" subject.

When Davies did a follow-up study, where he showed the same set of commercials to another set of college girls, he asked them afterward to rate how much they liked a variety of careers. Some careers involved math skills (such as being an engineer, computer scientist, and accountant), and some involved verbal skills (such as being a journalist, political scientist, and editor). Not only did the girls who watched the stereotypical commercials solve fewer math problems correctly, but they were also more interested in careers tapping verbal skills and less interested in careers using math skills compared to the girls who saw the neutral commercials.[6] It can be that simple. Two commercials and young women are already doing worse in math, not trying as hard at math, and rating math-based jobs as less interesting. Imagine what a lifetime of seeing those stereotypes can do.

# WHAT'S A PARENT TO DO?

Frankly, I find the research on stereotype threat to be incredibly discouraging: it is so easy to trigger, its effects are so widespread and meaningful, and it happens when I am not there to butt in. It all makes me feel a little powerless. I used an analogy earlier in the book about vaccinating our kids from stereotypes, but, to mix a few metaphors, it is also important to play defense against the storm of stereotypes that seem to be flung at our kids from every direction. Helping our kids survive the effects of stereotype threat is another way we can help them maximize their true potential.

Luckily, a lot of research has focused on some effective techniques you can use to help your kids be less vulnerable to stereotype threat. Sticking your head in the sand and hoping your kids are oblivious to the negative stereotypes concerning their group is not, however, on the list of tips. Remember: Your kids already know the stereotypes. I wish negative stereotypes about boys and girls didn't exist. But they do, and if your kid is old enough to be taking a test at school, he or she already knows them. Odds are, even young children are already taking a test under some conditions that trigger stereotype threat, so you might as well address the problem head-on.

The eight tips below can help protect your kids from stereotype threat. All have been shown by research studies to be effective and all are helpful for kids, regardless of the situation. They are good for every kid to hear, even in the absence of stereotype threat, but are especially helpful for a child doing work in a field of stereotype landmines.

1. De-emphasize gender. Encourage your kids to think of themselves in terms other than gender. There are two good ways to do this that reduce stereotype threat vulnerability. One is to encourage your kids to think of themselves as complex, multifaceted individuals. Have them create a self-concept map, where they draw a circle in the center of the page to represent themselves. Then draw as many smaller circles as possible coming off the main circle. In

each of the smaller circles, children should write a description of themselves (such as smart, funny, kind, good at soccer, like *SpongeBob SquarePants*, hate broccoli, fast runner, good at school, ticklish, and so on). They can include anything they can think of that describes themselves without including gender. The goal is to fill up the page with unique and specific qualities that make your child special. Focusing on the many parts of themselves that aren't linked to stereotypes helps reduce the power of those stereotypes.

The second way to reduce vulnerability to stereotype threat is to focus on the social identities that are not associated with stereotypes. For example, when you know your child is about to take a test in a stereotyped subject, prep them in the morning to think about being a third grader, or about being a member of their school or class, or about representing your family. Anything that can take the focus away from gender.

2. Reframe the task. When kids think the test they are taking is a measure of their true abilities, they are more vulnerable to stereotype threat (as though doing poorly on a test confirms that they have low math abilities). So remind them that one test can't tap their full abilities. The test is only a snapshot of how they are doing that day on those particular items. Also, remind them that the test is fair. Being reassured about the fairness of a test is a powerful way to help kids relax.

3. Discuss stereotype threat. Teach kids that they may feel anxious when they are taking a test, and that is a normal feeling that lots of people experience. Because there is a stereotype that boys aren't as good in school as girls (or fill in the blank for another stereotype), some boys think they have to do extra well on a test just to prove that stereotype wrong. But, remind him that the test isn't a perfect test of everything he is capable of and he shouldn't worry too much about it.

4. Encourage self-affirmation. Have your child think about the values, skills, and characteristics that are important to him or her and then take a few minutes to write a brief essay explaining why those values are important. This can be something like "It is important for me to be kind to my family ... (and why)" or "It is important for me to be a hard worker ... (and why)." Students who did this in a classroom, even though they were students who would normally be stereotyped, performed one-third of a grade point higher than students who didn't write about their values.[7] That's a difference that shows up on a report card.

5. Emphasize high standards, and assure kids that they are capable of meeting them. As I discussed in chapter 9, offering kids constructive feedback is important. This tells them that you know they can excel at what they work hard at. No one wants an unearned pat on the head. When kids do well, they know it. When they do poorly, they know that, too. No one likes condescension, even kids. So when their performance is subpar, offer feedback that helps them improve and then expect improvements. This is a powerful message about your belief in your child's capacity to be great. This is much more powerful than a hollow "Good job."

6. Provide competent role models. Point out men and women who excel at whatever they are not "supposed" to excel at. Use examples of people you know, and point out the examples you see on TV, in movies, or in books. These examples can be real people or fictional characters. Point out women who excel at math to girls. Point out men who excel at writing to boys. Have children read short stories of men and women who excel despite the stereotypes. Encourage your children to think about these high-achieving individuals when they are taking a test.

7. Provide alternative explanations for anxiety. One of the primary reasons stereotype threat reduces performance is that the ensuing anxiety distracts a student from the task at hand. So one

way to keep performance high is to help kids explain away the anxiety. For example, one study taught middle school students about the difficulties of transitioning to middle school and about the anxiety and worry that many students feel in their classes. They emphasized that this was normal and temporary and would get better over time. Those students were no longer vulnerable to stereotype threat. Some kids have been taught that the anxiety they feel may actually boost their performance (in other words, it is good anxiety). Those kids were also protected from stereotype threat.

8. Teach that intelligence comes from trying hard, rather than innate talents. People have one of two views of intelligence. Some people think it is fixed and can never change. You are either born with a lot or a little of it. If you are born with a lot of it, hooray! You will do well in school. Everyone else, sorry about your luck. Other people think intelligence can be increased with hard work, studying, and focus on academics. They think of intelligence like a muscle that gets stronger with work. Kids who have the "muscle" theory of intelligence are protected from stereotype threat. They know that they may have a bad test grade one day but can keep working at it and improve. One test doesn't reveal the beginning and end of their abilities. So teach your kids that effort is more important than "being smart." Not only does thinking of intelligence as a muscle protect kids from stereotype threat, but thinking of intelligence as a fixed quantity can also actually exacerbate stereotype threat. Those kids are extra vulnerable to the nasty effects of stereotypes. A little side note: Culturally, American kids, parents, and teachers typically view intelligence as something innate. We talk about people being "smart" and "not so smart." As a group, Chinese kids, parents, and teachers view intelligence as more malleable, increasing with work and effort. Some education researchers argue that this basic difference explains why Chinese students do so much better at school than American students.

This belief in the value of effort leads students to work hard, never lose motivation, and stick with a challenging problem until it is solved.

## THE FINAL FOUR:
## WHAT ARE THE KEY ISSUES?

- Being concerned with confirming a negative stereotype can actually lead kids to do worse on the task at hand. This is called stereotype threat—in other words, the mere existence of the stereotype threatens their ability to do well.

- All kids (and adults) are vulnerable to stereotype threat in certain situations. Any situation that triggers children to think about their gender, the stereotypes associated with their gender, or the test as a reflection of their abilities can lead to anxiety, decreases in working memory, stress, and a negative internal dialogue (those "I can't do this" thoughts). All this extra mental baggage drags down performance just enough to be noticeable.

- Over time, kids try to avoid stereotype threat. This leads them to pull out of those subjects associated with negative stereotypes and into the more "appropriate" subjects. This is why so many women say "I am not a math person" and why so many men never read for pleasure. Avoiding stereotypes can even direct kids into stereotypical career paths.

- Parents can do a lot to help protect kids from stereotype threat, but to do that, parents have to address the problem head-on and not assume kids are oblivious to stereotypes.

## CHAPTER 11

# Separate but Equal? An Old Problem Is New Again

**I saved this chapter for last because** it is the issue that surprises—and frustrates—me the most. It is an issue that shows a big disconnect between what research shows us and what policymakers decide to do. I think you too will be shocked by what is a rapidly growing trend in public education in the United States. Before I explain this trend, and the consequences for children, take this brief quiz.

Guess the decade of the following quotes:

1. "Women prefer to follow, and are willing to do so without knowing any reason for doing such action." "Boys do more original work in math." "Girls are not interested in scientific abstractions and experiments."

2. "Girls tend to prefer to have things conceptualized in usable, everyday language, replete with concrete details." "Males are not

really interested in rote, repetitive, mundane exercises, compared with creative hands-on projects that culminate in something with a different level of understanding.... You can put a group of girls doing a science lab, and they're going to follow the directions, they're going to go through the process and may not even understand what happened in the science lab, but they got the right answers."

The sentiment of these statements is the same. Girls can follow directions just fine, just don't give them anything abstract. They may go through the steps without ever knowing exactly what they are doing.

Hopefully, you guessed these quotations originated from some time in the early twentieth century. If so, you are partially correct. The first set of quotations came from around 1910, when the country was debating whether girls should attend regular high schools instead of schools that simply taught domestic skills.[1] At that time, girls were being prepared for futures as wives and mothers, and science and mathematics were simply unnecessary—perhaps even harmful—subjects to learn. Prominent thinkers of the time, such as Dr. Edward Clarke of Harvard Medical School, thought that girls had a finite amount of energy and that blood flow that went to the brain would literally drain the ovaries. They were concerned that women who became too educated would lose the ability to bear children, and even if they had children, would be too pedantic to raise them properly.

But unfortunately, you are not entirely correct if you guessed the early twentieth century. The second set of quotations came from 2006. Yes, 2006, the same year I was setting up a Facebook account, learning to text message, and miraculously had both a baby and an education. Think the quotation is from some quack off the street with no influence? No, it's from a school superintendent in Wisconsin.[2]

Or maybe you think the second set of quotations was taken out of context and not meant for public ears? Unfortunately, that isn't the case, either. Here are some more gems, from different people—these taken from court depositions of middle school math and science teachers (coincedentally all men) in the 2010 court case of A.N.A. v. Breckinridge County Public School District.[3]

- "Boys are capable of higher thought processes, so if I can give them a tough problem, then they can really challenge one another. As the Bible says, 'Iron sharpens iron,' so our minds are going to go ahead and sharpen one another."

- "The boys, generally, are capable of abstract thought, while girls in most cases needed hands-on demonstrative props to understand the same mathematical concepts."

- "I play lots of review games with my boys so they can get up and move, where the girls would rather I just ask questions and they can write down the answers."

- "Boys are better than girls in math because boys' bodies receive daily surges of testosterone, whereas girls don't understand mathematical theory very well except for a few days a month when their estrogen is surging."

This is the growing trend in education—these types of descriptions of boys and girls. These quotations (from school teachers and officials) are specifically being used to justify segregating public school kids into single-sex classes, just as we did in 1910. The argument is that boys and girls learn so differently, because of supposed brain-based differences, that they must be taught in different classrooms. In the States, there is a rapid growth of single-sex classrooms, all based on these views of boys' and girls' abilities. After reading page after page of these comments, I usually need a sedative.

## REGRESSION AFTER RECESSION

In the United States in 2001, the Elementary and Secondary Education Act was reauthorized, famously referred to as No Child Left Behind (NCLB). When NCLB was passed, an important change was made in how American public schools could operate. To push schools to be more "innovative," public schools were allowed to offer same-sex schools and classrooms. This marked an important change in educational policy, reversing the previous ban on gender segregation in public schools.

It is hard to track exactly how many schools are now single sex. The National Association for Choice in Education (which used to be called National Association for Single-Sex Schools in Public Education) used to track single-sex public schools in the United States. As of 2011, more than five hundred public schools in forty U.S. states were segregated by gender.[4] But they refuse to release those numbers anymore, in part because the ACLU kept suing the schools for violating the Constitution's ban on gender discrimination. Regardless, these numbers seem to underestimate the growing trend. The Gurian Institute, which indoctrinates teachers about these supposed gender differences and makes drastically different educational recommendations for boys and girls, has trained over fifty thousand teachers in more than two thousand school districts. It seems safe to say that gender segregation in public schools, rationalized because of supposed brain differences between boys and girls, has gone mainstream.

This assumption that boys and girls learn differently—and therefore must be taught separately—seems to stem from a well-meaning attempt to improve the quality of education. As we are repeatedly reminded in the media, American schools trail behind schools in almost every other country. In a comparison of math achievement scores of high school students across thirty countries, American students are outperformed by twenty-three of the other twenty-nine countries.[5] The longer American students are in school, the more they lag behind their international peers. In fourth grade, American students are top competitors. But by eighth grade, bigger differences emerge, and by high school, American students are at the bottom of the pile.

Teachers and school administrators are understandably frustrated and looking anywhere for solutions for this pervasive low achievement. Since they can't exactly get a major influx of government funding just because they ask nicely, they have to look for simple (read: inexpensive) solutions. They turn to what seems like a logical answer. Boys and girls act differently in school. Therefore, they must be inherently different in learning styles as well. Boys do better in math and girls do better in reading. The inference is that they must be hardwired differently (this way of thinking is why *Men Are from Mars, Women Are from Venus* is such a best seller). Maybe if teaching is differentially tailored to boys and girls, everyone's achievement will improve. At least that is how the thinking seems to go. And the folks making money by pushing single-sex schools via their training institutes and workshops are eager to train teachers on the "brain-based" differences between boys and girls (for a small fee, of course). So the problem is low achievement in schools. The solution is to blame gender.

To fully understand what is happening in school districts around the country, we need to investigate this trend. In this chapter, I outline some of the arguments in favor of single-sex public schools and describe some of the specific educational recommendations that are currently being implemented in these schools. I then talk about whether these schools are effective or not (and why it is hard to tell). I also discuss some of the consequences for children of attending these schools. I end with practical recommendations for parents, based on your own school district.

## THE ARGUMENTS FOR
## SEGREGATED SCHOOLS

As I mentioned, one of the major arguments for single-sex public schools is that boys and girls are hardwired differently and thus must be taught separately. I have hopefully shed some light on this misguided issue in this book. I won't rehash every myth about gender that is being used to justify teaching boys and girls differently. For example, one popular claim is the supposed difference in the corpus callosum, which two meta-analyses have completely refuted and called a "myth."

Much of that is covered in chapters 5, 6, and 7. Indeed, one reason I spent so much time on these myths of gender differences is because they are being used to shape educational policy. To illustrate the point, I will detail one specific claim that is used to argue for different classrooms for boys and girls.

One difference between boys and girls—one reason they need different classrooms—is because girls supposedly have heightened sensory capacities compared to boys. Proponents of these brain-based differences (most notably, Leonard Sax) tell teachers that girls have very sensitive hearing and vision compared to boys, so their classrooms should be dimmer and teachers should talk to them in softer voices. A teacher needs to talk loudly to a boy, but these loud voices would be overwhelming to the delicate female ear. They encourage teachers of girls to sit in dim rooms and whisper and teachers of boys to stand in bright rooms and yell—seriously.[6] If I were one of these girls in a dim, quiet room, math time would devolve into naptime.

What does the research really show? First, when you look across all of the studies on the topic, newborn girls have more sensitive hearing than boys in five of the thirteen different experiments. In the other eight studies, there were no differences.[7] Second, when a difference is found, it is incredibly tiny and not at all related to regular hearing. To give you a sense of the difference, when a truck backs up and begins to beep, that beep's frequency is about 1000 Hz. At that level, women can hear about one decibel better than men. That difference disappears at normal conversation levels in a classroom (which are usually at about sixty decibels). Also, the difference refers to what people can detect at their threshold for hearing, not how sensitive they are to regular noise levels. As Dennis McFadden, an expert in auditory perception and professor emeritus at the University of Texas at Austin, said, "This verges on the absurd ... Arguing for separate schools because of the small sex difference in hearing is just dopey."[8] Mark Liberman, the professor of linguistics at Penn, called it "preposterous."[9]

Despite neuroscientists stringently disagreeing with these

interpretations of the research, many argue that these "biological gender differences" necessitate teaching boys and girls in different classes using very different teaching strategies. But, as described in chapter 5, boys and girls have largely overlapping distributions, and even legitimate gender differences are based on small effect sizes. We know that boys differ from other boys and girls differ from other girls more than boys as a group differ from girls as a group.

Splitting everyone up simply based on gender and then teaching to some stereotyped version of a boy or a girl overlooks all this variability. One popular reason for segregating boys and girls is based on boys' greater activity level (which, if you remember from chapter 4, starts as a small difference in infancy and gets bigger with age and reinforcement). The recommendation is that boys should not have chairs and desks but should be allowed to move around throughout the day throwing balls (girls, however, are expected to sit quietly at their desks). Even though there is an actual difference in activity level, the difference is small and overlooks the fact that most boys and girls differ from the hypothetical "average" boy or girl.

It would be one thing if schools tested everyone's activity levels and then split kids into "Active Classroom" and "Chilled-Out Classroom" or actually tested hearing sensitivity and divided everyone into the "Yellers" and the "Whisperers." In other words, if the rationale for segregating by gender is that children with certain traits need different types of teaching, they should split up the classrooms based on the traits, not gender. Then, at least, the different classrooms would be based on actual differences instead of stereotyped ones.

Another argument for segregating boys and girls into different classrooms is that boys and girls have different preferences and interests. Some single-sex public classrooms have boys writing about where in the world they would most like to go hunting or drive on a racetrack and girls writing about their dream wedding dress or their ideal birthday party. In other schools, girls read *Emma* and boys read *Huck Finn*. Some schools are using hunting analogies in lessons for boys and dishwashing analogies for girls. Boys are often given quizzes about bikes, while girls are quizzed on bracelets.[10] The idea is that education should cater to kids' interests, and because those interests differ by gender, classes should differ by gender, too.

Frankly, my daughter is currently interested in *SpongeBob SquarePants* and Webkinz. Part of why she goes to school is to expand her interests. I don't want a school to cater to every whim of my nine-year-old. Otherwise, she would talk about cartoons all day, stop reading when she got bored, and interrupt the teacher to tell a fart joke. It's like the parents who only feed their children chicken nuggets and macaroni and cheese. Yes, that is what the kids like. But part of the job of parenting is to cover the basic food groups and expand their tastes so that as adults they have a reasonable palate and know how to recognize a vegetable. School should not just cater to kids' tastes, either. School should also help expand their intellectual palates. That means boys should read books with lead female characters and girls should read Mark Twain.

An additional argument for segregating kids by gender is that boys sometimes harass girls and teachers may be sexist toward their students. This is a feminist argument asserting that there is sexism within schools and we should shield kids from it. There is, indeed, harassment within schools. Our research shows that more than 90 percent of middle and high school girls have been sexually harassed by a boy at some point.[11] And yes, teachers sometimes show bias toward one gender or the other. Often boys get in trouble for an offense that is ignored when a girl perpetrates it. But as Rebecca Bigler, executive director of the American Council for Co-Educational Schooling, frequently says, "The solution to sexism in schools isn't to remove the 'sex' from the classroom; it should be to remove the 'ism.' Fix the unfairness; don't simply ignore the problem by pretending the other gender doesn't exist."[12]

## DO SEGREGATED SCHOOLS WORK?

Even if the reasons for single-sex schools are pretty bogus (that's the scientific term!), they could still be effective. Many, many people have tried to test the effectiveness of single-sex schools, and there are many studies out there to pick from. The problem is that evaluating whether single-sex schools are better or worse for kids' academic lives is difficult. They can't be adequately examined for their effectiveness because we can't randomly assign some kids to attend a single-sex school and some kids to attend a mixed-sex school. There are a lot of selection effects by kids, parents, and the schools that muddy the water. In other words, there are a lot of preexisting differences between kids who attend a single-sex school (and their parents) and kids who attend a mixed-sex school (and their parents) that make them difficult compare.

For example, kids who want to attend a single-sex school will often thrive there because they were unhappy at their mixed-sex school. This has nothing to do with gender per se. Letting kids pick their own school contributes to their success.

Parents who send their child to a single-sex school also differ from other parents. First, they believe in the effectiveness of single-sex education. And we know how powerful parents' beliefs are in shaping their children's outcomes (see chapters 8 and 9). Second, for a child to attend a single-sex school, parents typically have to seek out the school, fill out an application, and arrange transportation to the school (and, if it's a private school, pay tuition). Because their child needs to maintain good grades to stay in the school, parents are involved in homework and they help out at the school. This requires a high level of parent involvement and resources. Parents who are very involved in their child's education, and who have financial and intellectual resources, have kids who academically succeed, wherever they go.

Third, if parents choose to send their kid to a single-sex school, they have made a commitment to that choice. We know that once people commit to a choice and believe in something, they only seek out and remember information that fits their belief and they misremember other information (see chapters 4, 8, and 9). Of course, their interpretation of their child's single-sex school is going be positive.

Finally, single-sex schools can select the types of kids who attend their school, and they are often selective about who they let through the doors. Research has shown that even when the single-sex schools claim they select children randomly through a lottery system, the selected students start out with higher grades than the rejected students.[13] Starting out with the highest achievers is an easy way to seem really effective (this is true for private schools as well). Single-sex schools, whether public or private, can also expel low-performing kids, which makes their test scores look high in ways that regular schools can't (I know lots of public school teachers who would secretly love to boot the trouble-making, low-achieving students.)

All of these selection biases mean that children who attend (and stay at) a single-sex school are already different than children who attend a mixed-sex school, before they attend a day of school. Then, once the school year starts, single-sex schools often do a lot of extra work that education experts say is beneficial for all students. For example, when public schools convert from mixed sex to single sex, they also increase their emphasis on academics—often assigning more homework, making the school day longer, adding tutors and mentors, requiring uniforms, and bringing in motivational speakers and role models.

Teachers also have high expectations for the students who go to these special "innovative" schools. Like parents making choices for their children, teachers also choose to teach at a single-sex school because they believe in its effectiveness. The expectations influence everything. As an example, in one school focused on African-American students, they found that the teachers in the single-sex classrooms gave the students higher grades than teachers in the mixed-sex classrooms, although their standardized test scores didn't differ at all.[14] In other words, teachers were rating the single-sex kids higher, even though they weren't actually higher. Although this is surely unintentional, it means that studies of school effectiveness are really measuring teachers' expectations and not single-sex schools per se. In many ways, single-sex schools work like a placebo—a sugar pill of education—eliciting the very behaviors everyone expects.

Considering all of these factors in favor of single-sex education, it is surprising that these schools aren't overwhelmingly effective. The U.S. Department of Education (the same department that allowed these schools to begin with), in their analysis of the effectiveness of single-sex schools versus mixed-sex schools, called the findings "equivocal." Basically, 35 percent of the existing studies found single-sex schools beneficial, but 53 percent of the studies found no difference between the types of schools.[15] Again, this is surprising considering all of the reasons that single-sex students should be superstars. Rosemary Salomone, a big advocate for single-sex schools, called findings about their effectiveness "tentative" and "not sufficiently weighty to yield definitive conclusions," and said there is "little conclusive evidence."[16] A large Canadian project to evaluate single-sex schools, ironically titled "Single-Sex Schooling: Final Report," called the studies "inconclusive."[17]

Luckily, other studies have probed a little deeper.[18] When you look carefully, the effectiveness of single-sex schools seems to come from the quality of education and the quality of peers. When researchers compared students' achievement from a selective single-sex school to a comparable mixed-sex magnet school (schools with similar selectivity in who they admitted and a similar emphasis on academics), the students performed exactly the same. Attending an academically rigorous school with other motivated, bright kids is the key for anyone to do well in school. It seems that when single-sex schools do look great, it is because of their stringent admission policies, bright student body, and academic rigor; gender is irrelevant.

# The Real Science of Learning

We know a lot about the science of learning. But what helps kids learn and how can we maximize their learning environment? Notice that the list below doesn't rest on gender as an explanation anywhere. Use this list to help your kids study and learn better. Check to see whether your child's teacher is using the best learning strategies.

1. Kids need associated ideas to be presented together. Ideas that need to be linked with one another (such as a picture and its label) should be presented side-by-side. That way, the brain can process them at the exact same time. Also, explanations of events should be given when the event is depicted rather than many minutes, hours, or days later.

2. Whenever a new concept is first introduced, kids should first visualize a picture of the concept. They should then be given a hands-on opportunity to concretely manipulate the new concept or observe how it functions over time. This is called perceptual-motor experience. It is particularly important when there is a need for precision, such as getting directions to find a spatial location. This is much better than teaching math by just writing a formula on the board. For example, instead of learning fractions by writing them on a piece of paper, have the child slice a pie into the needed units. Hands-on beats an abstract formula any day, for everyone.

3. Kids remember information better when it comes in multiple ways using as many senses as possible. Information should be presented with words and pictures, via computers and lectures, and using kids' auditory, visual, and tactile senses. The trick is to do this without making things too cluttered. Distracting, irrelevant details, even if they look cool, can slow down learning.

4. Frequent, regularly spaced testing on new material is actually helpful (this is different than frequent standardized testing). Kids should be given feedback about what they got right or wrong right after the test to help clarify what they didn't understand. This serves as a guide for learning, helps students pace their studying, and reduces forgetting. They also need to know that

this learned material will be repeatedly tested. The best kinds of tests are essay tests or free recall tests in place of multiple choice tests where kids just have to pick out the best answer.

5. Learning should be spaced out, not crammed together. Professor Nate Kornell, a cognitive psychologist at Williams College, has shown time and again the value of spacing out the learning and studying process. In one experimental study, he had some students study a stack of flashcards over the course of a week versus other students who cram-studied the flashcards over one long day (you all remember those days from school). Students who spaced out their learning did 30 percent better than the crammers. This was effective for 90 percent of the learners.[19]

6. Kids should be encouraged to outline, integrate, and synthesize information, instead of just rereading a book over and over. Strategies that require learners to be actively engaged with the material produce better long-term memory results than the passive act of reading. Writing out an outline of a chapter after reading it is a good way to turn passive learning into active learning. It is helpful if children test themselves as they go, and restate in their own words what they are learning.

7. Kids need many examples to learn new information. Stories and other forms of narrative are great because they are easier to read, comprehend, and remember than other types of materials. Stories have concrete characters that can be visualized, there is a plot to engage the imagination, and emotions and actions can help the students personally relate to the material. Capturing a child's attention is a big part of the learning process. When abstract concepts are being taught, give the students multiple concrete examples.

8. Learning that can be tied to something that kids care about is most effective. For example, helping students understand scientific principles by trying to fix pollution in their city is both concrete and interesting for students. Activities that are organized around solving a practical problem can teach both the specific material and general problem-solving strategies.

9. Kids should be asked for deep explanations of the material. They should be asked why, how, what-if, and what-if-not questions. These are better than more shallow questions that require the learner to simply fill in missing words, such as who, what, where, and when. Training your kids to ask deep questions helps them better learn the material.

There are many other ways to improve learning at home and school that I encourage you to investigate. Many of these suggestions are taken from Life Long Learning at Work and Home, a research initiative at the University of Memphis. Visit their website for more information and resources: http://psyc.memphis.edu/learning. What is apparent in all of the research on learning is that there is no need to address gender.

## NO HARM, NO FOUL?

Okay, so maybe single-sex public schools don't exactly fix every educational ailment, but one could argue that they provide a choice, and choices are good. Who cares about single-sex schools existing alongside mixed-sex schools, as long as they do no harm? Well, good solid empirical evidence suggests they do some harm, both cognitively and socially.

Any kind of segregated education, especially education that is designed to be stereotypical, molds children into those very stereotypes. Much of chapter 6 discussed how our experiences shape our brains. All of that research suggests that if we provide entirely different educations for boys and girls based on supposed stereotypical differences, then we literally create differences in the brain. Imagine a science teacher who assumes girls are not interested in visual-spatial tasks, instead preferring verbal tasks. Rather than creating a lesson plan that involves creating a molecule out of sugar cubes and toothpicks, he just describes the molecule to the girls. Enough of those stereotypical experiences add up to real differences. Studies described earlier in the book show that girls who practice manipulating shapes have spatial abilities that match those of boys. But, if children never get the opportunity to practice those skills, those neurons suffer the same use-it-or-lose-it pruning that happens throughout childhood. Because of misguided segregation and different types of teaching, what began as a stereotype becomes a reality.

Single-sex schools are also a breeding ground for stereotype threat (described in chapter 10). Mounds of research clearly and consistently show that one way to reduce kids' performance on a stereotyped task is to make them think about their gender. What's an effective way to ensure their gender is salient throughout the day? Make the entire class day based on gender. Segregation into single-sex classrooms doesn't decrease thoughts of gender; it makes everything dependent on gender. These classrooms are a textbook condition for how to work under constant stereotype threat.

These stereotypical segregated schools also do harm on the social side of education. For example, in California, in 1997, Governor Pete Wilson established six pairs of single-sex "academies" (a term sometimes used for schools within a school). This was funded by a half-million-dollar state grant. Not only did they make the schools single sex, but they also gave them extra computers, field trips, and smaller class sizes. The problem was that outside people (funded by the Ford Foundation) actually came to the schools to evaluate how the program was going.

What they found was that the segregation actually "pitted boys and girls against one another and reinforced gender stereotypes."[20] They found that, whenever they put the boys and girls together, sexual harassment toward girls (such as hearing harassing comments and being touched against their wishes) spiked. It was so clear that the programs were not working as intended that five of the academies were shut down within three years. Other findings show similar trends, with boys being rowdy, getting in fights more often, and getting bullied more often in all-boy classes.

Not only do these classrooms foster stereotypical behavior, but they also send powerful messages about the differences between boys and girls. What are children told about segregation? They are told that boys and girls are totally different from each other and therefore need different classrooms. But this is not true. If boys are taught that they lag behind girls in their class in reading and thus need to be taught in a different class, is that true? No. Does every boy lag behind every girl in reading? Of course not. But splitting boys and girls into different classrooms implies that all boys differ from all girls. That is the message kids learn.

Worse is that children's exposure to segregation can actually create stereotypes. Children who grow up in an environment in which one group of people work and play in isolation from another group develop stereotypes and biases. Imagine for a minute that some children attend schools or classes based on their weight. Overweight children and normal weight children have their own separate classes or even schools. Indeed, overweight children are often stigmatized by their peers and, one might argue, should be protected from bullying by being placed in classes with only other overweight children. We could have a skinny school and a fat school. Would that be a good idea? What would happen to children's stereotypes and prejudices about weight in an education system that used weight segregation? I bet the skinny kids wouldn't like the overweight kids, and the feeling would be mutual. Segregation doesn't end stereotyping—it fuels it.

This isn't exactly the first time we've tried out segregation, either. For much of American history, race segregation was the norm. And we heard many of the same reasons that people are now using for segregation by gender. We are just so different.... It is to protect the kids.... There would be so much hostility, it could never work. But in 1954, the U.S. Supreme Court realized that separate could never truly be equal, that separate always leads to more stereotypes, that a diverse world calls for a diverse classroom.

Diane Halpern, a Trustee Professor of Psychology at Claremont McKenna College, is the former president of the American Psychological Association. She has been called to testify before Congress on several issues related to education. She has also written a textbook (now in its fourth edition) called *Sex Differences in Cognitive Abilities*. She recently provided expert testimony in some of the court cases questioning the legality of these new public single-sex schools. She argues, forcefully, that the research does not justify single-sex education. She urges people to realize that it will exacerbate the problems in education, not reduce them. Here is her statement in her court testimony:

> Our students are entering a world with global problems that include pollution, poverty, racism, and terrorism, just to name a few. We need to improve high school graduation rates, literacy levels, and critical thinking skills for those students who are slipping through the chasms in our educational system. There are many critical challenges that our schools must face and no evidence that single-sex education will fix what is broken . . . Our students need more diversity in their everyday lives and learning environments, including learning with and from girls and boys. How else can we prepare them to work together?[21]

Amen.

## WHAT CAN PARENTS DO?

My hope is that you take everything from this book, see how misguided it is to base educational policy on stereotypes, and get a little pissed off, too. I hope you spread the word when you hear your friends talking about how "boys and girls learn differently." I hope parents of girls are irritated that educators think your daughter can't learn an abstract concept. Get angry that some schools assume girls can't take timed tests because they are overly stressful for delicate girls (how they are supposed to take the SATs, I don't know). I hope parents of boys are irritated that educators think your son is so impulsive and unmanageable that he isn't allowed to sit down during the school day. Get mad that teachers aren't supposed to smile at your son because he will read that as a sign of weakness.

If this impacts your child's school district, which it is likely to in the next few years if the trend continues, take action. The exact recommendations depend on your own situation, though. If your child's school is mixed sex, but you hear through the grapevine that they are in favor of a change to single sex (this is what's happening in my own school district), here are some actions you can take:

1. Email the district superintendent's office and ask about the future plans for schools. The more often they hear directly from parents, the better. He or she may or may not respond (it sometimes depends on how large the school district is), but the email will get sent to someone. If you don't get a response, try again.

2. Recommend *Pink Brain, Blue Brain* to them or even this book. Encourage them to investigate the scientific claims showing that boys and girls learn differently. The science just isn't there.

3. Direct them to the ACLU's web page (www.aclu.org/womens-rights/sex-segregated-schools-separate-and-unequal) about single-sex public schools. Many schools are now facing lawsuits because the legality of these schools is being called into question.

If your child's public school is terrible and there is a substantially better single-sex school option, take these actions:

1. Before enrolling your child in a single-sex school, make sure that you can switch back to your original school if you are unhappy with the choice. The single-sex school may look good from the brochure but really be a hotbed of stereotypes. Some all-girls schools (for example, the Young Women's Leadership School in New York) don't even offer advanced math classes for the girls. They don't exactly advertise this on their website.

2. Try to ensure that the rest of your child's world is gender diverse. Enroll them in mixed-gender team sports and extracurricular activities, take vacations with other kids of both genders, and expose them to successful male and female role models.

3. Explicitly address the disadvantages of segregated schooling. Explain how stereotypes may increase because of their school. Explain how stereotype threat may impact their academic performance. Addressing these issues head-on helps reduce their impact.

If you think that boys and girls are hardwired differently from birth and need different educational strategies . . . turn to page 1 and start again.

## THE FINAL FOUR: WHAT ARE THE KEY ISSUES?

- There is a growing trend in the United States to offer single-sex public schools because of the misguided assumption that boys and girls learn so differently that they need to be taught separately.

- Many of these schools are teaching boys and girls on the basis of gender stereotypes (such as girls can't learn abstract concepts and boys can only learn when competing with one another). These schools overlook the natural overlap between boys and girls. Shocking news: All boys don't learn the same way and all girls don't learn the same way.

- Not only are single-sex schools ineffective, but they can also mold kids into the very stereotypes they oppose. Plus, being educated in a segregated school (especially when that school is based on stereotypic teaching) only serves to increase kids' beliefs in the stereotypes.

- This is a growing trend in schools, and so it is likely to come to a school near you. Take action. Parents need to be engaged in how educational policy is shaped, and that action needs to be based on real science, not stereotypes.

# Dropping the Stereotypes and Picking Your Battles

**As a parent, it is hard not to be frustrated** when you think about our cultural obsession with gender. We developmental psychologists, know a lot about children and their gender. We know that there are a few differences between boys and girls when they are born, but most of those differences are quite small. We know that stereotypes take over really early on—from the moment the little one enters the world—and never let go. We know that parents shape children in ways that fit with stereotypes even when it is unintentional, and kids stereotype themselves even when parents try to fight it. We also know that stereotypes limit the potential that kids are born with. Smart, math-loving girls drop out of math tracks and take English lit. Sensitive, sweet-natured boys learn to hide their emotions and act tough. Strong, athletic girls eventually go on a diet and feel bad about their bodies. Boys struggle through school in silence because asking for help is a sign of weakness.

The science is clear: the stereotype usually trumps biology in shaping who we become. And even though those stereotypes are hard to fight, I urge you to try to fight them anyway. I think it is a good fight and ultimately worth it. Individuals with both masculine and feminine traits (who are assertive, independent, nurturing, and empathetic) do better the rest of their lives. They are happier, less likely to be depressed, and more likely to have fulfilling careers. They have happier family lives, find parenting more rewarding, and have healthier bodies. I know those are goals I have for my own kids.

If nothing else, I hope you put this book down and do two things. First, relegate gender to where it belongs, as just one of the many characteristics of your kids. Try to think of it as no different than hair color or height. I think height makes a great analogy. I am 5'3". I am short, even for a woman. My height is biological, obvious, and unchangeable. It affects some of the things I do. For example, I need help pushing my suitcase into the overhead bin of an airplane. But if no one is around, I climb on the seat in front of me and give it a heave. I need a step ladder to reach the top cabinets. But I am also adept at climbing on the countertop to get what I need. Granted, my height lowered my odds of being a basketball superstar. It didn't prevent me from achieving basketball greatness (the star of my high school basketball team was just as short as me); I just would have had to work harder at it compared to someone six feet tall.

Gender should be treated similarly. It is biological, obvious, and unchangeable. It can push the odds of our doing a behavior in one direction or another. One child is more likely to speak earlier if she is a girl. One child is more likely to be aggressive if he is a boy. But nothing is hard and fast, or impossible. My height doesn't determine everything about me. It is just part of who I am. So is my gender. No more, no less.

The second thing I hope you do is alter some of the things you do as a parent. You don't have to go wild and crazy, just make some tweaks. Trust me, I am no revolutionary. No one has ever called me militant. However, I am sneaky and subversive, and I pick my battles.

Here are the top three parenting choices I make on a regular basis:

1. I throw out or donate a lot of clothes and toys that are stereotypical. I recently donated a shirt that said "I love shopping" and I always donate Barbies, Bratz dolls, and Monster High dolls. Just because someone gave my child a gift doesn't mean I have to allow that gift to influence her. And toys and clothes and the messages they convey do influence our kids. I also say no to a lot of TV shows and movies. Many are stereotypical, and I don't mind saying, "No, I don't like the messages in that movie."

2. I alter the language I use with my kids. I don't call them "pretty girls" or "big girls." I just call them kids. I don't use other people's gender either when I talk. I just pick a more descriptive label. Kids, parents, police officer, teacher, clerk, doctor. It isn't hard. I would mention the gender if I was asked, or if it was really relevant, but it usually isn't.

3. I stop my kids from using their own stereotypes. When they say something stereotypical, I correct it. And importantly, I comment on what I see in the world. When other adults say something stereotypical, I mention it to my kids and correct it in private.

Here are a few assumptions I hope you'll avoid after reading this book:

1. Don't assume toys are just for fun and that movies and TV are only mindless entertainment. They all influence children's views of themselves and the world. Just because it is meant to be funny doesn't mean you should take it lightly.

2. Don't assume that you don't have influence in the face of media, culture, and well-meaning grandmas. You just have to decide to be the loudest voice above the din.

3. Don't assume anything about your child (what he or she will like, dislike, excel at, or act like) solely on the basis of his or her gender. If given the chance, individuals vary greatly, and not along gendered lines. If you start with an open mind at the nursery, your kids can grow up to be far more interesting than a simple stereotype.

At the end of the day, am I successful in my attempt to reduce how stereotypes affect my own kids? It's hard to say. I know Maya's favorite subject is math and she doesn't think her appearance is the most important thing about her (I have seen her leave the house, I know this is true). She knows how to use a hammer and how to feed a baby. She stands up forcefully to bullies and comforts her friends when they are sad. I know Grace's teacher commented the other day, "I love how Grace loves such diverse toys." She loves to wear her Minnie Mouse dress, especially with her firefighter helmet. She is strong and likes to climb. She says she wants to be a firefighter like her dad, but she also likes her toenails painted. Her favorite toys are cars and balls, especially when they are pink.

It isn't about denying that children are girls or boys. It is about children not being defined by gender. My girls are unique, very different from one another. I recognize that variability and uniqueness in them. It is about reducing the stereotypes that harm them and strengthening the traits that are good for everyone. And it is about allowing their unique strengths to shine through.

For this to happen, you have to set the stage at birth and address it head-on from that time on. The pink or blue worlds start early and don't go away on their own. Setting a good example in your own house is great, but it isn't enough. Encourage everyone to pay a little more attention to the influence of gender stereotypes and be a little more irritated by it. That is how change happens.

# Notes

## Chapter 2

1. Bigler, Rebecca S. "The Role of Classification Skill in Moderating Environmental Influences on Children's Gender Stereotyping: A Study of the Functional Use of Gender in the Classroom." *Child Development* 66 (1995): 1072–1087.
2. Jewell, Jennifer A., and Christia Spears Brown. "Relations Among Gender Typicality, Peer Relations, and Mental Health During Early Adolescence." *Social Development* 23 (2013): 137–156.
3. Bigler, Rebecca S., Christia Spears Brown, and Marc Markell. "When Groups Are Not Created Equal: Effects of Group Status on the Formation of Intergroup Attitudes in Children." *Child Development* 72 (2001): 1151–1162.
4. Brown, Christia Spears, and Rebecca S. Bigler. "Effects of Minority Status in the Classroom on Children's Intergroup Attitudes." *Journal of Experimental Child Psychology* 83 (2002): 77–110.
5. Patterson, Meagan M., and Rebecca S. Bigler. "Preschool Children's Attention to Environmental Messages about Groups: Social Categorization and the Origins of Intergroup Bias." *Child Development* 77.4 (2006): 847-860.
6. Taylor, Marianne G., Marjorie Rhodes, and Susan A. Gelman. "Boys Will Be Boys; Cows Will Be Cows: Children's Essentialist Reasoning about Gender Categories and Animal Species." *Child Development* 80 (2009): 461–481.
7. Liben, Lynn S., Rebecca S. Bigler, and Holleen R. Krogh. "Language at Work: Children's Gendered Interpretations of Occupational Titles." *Child Development* 73 (2002): 810–828.
8. DeLoache, Judy S., Deborah J. Cassidy, and C. Jan Carpenter. "The Three Bears Are All Boys: Mothers' Gender Labeling of Neutral Picture Book Characters." *Sex Roles* 17.3–4 (1987): 163–178.
9. Oskamp, Stuart, Karen Kaufman, and Lianna Atchison Wolterbeek. "Gender Role Portrayals in Preschool Picture Books." *Journal of Social Behavior and Personality* 11.5 (1996): 27–39.
10. Martin, Carol Lynn, and Charles F. Halverson Jr. "The Effects of Sex-typing Schemas on Young Children's Memory." *Child Development* (1983): 563–574.
11. Leaper, Campbell, Kristin J. Anderson, and Paul Sanders. "Moderators of Gender Effects on Parents' Talk to Their Children: A Meta-analysis." *Developmental Psychology* 34.1 (1998): 3.
12. Chang, Alicia, Catherine M. Sandhofer, and Christia S. Brown. "Gender Biases in Early Number Exposure to Preschool-aged Children." *Journal of Language and Social Psychology* 30.4 (2011): 440-450.

## Chapter 3

1. Leinbach, Mary Driver, and Beverly I. Fagot. "Categorical Habituation to Male and Female Faces: Gender Schematic Processing in Infancy." *Infant Behavior and Development* 16 (1993): 317–332.
2. Ibid.

3. Reicher, Steven. "Biography of Henri Tajfel (1919–1982)." European Association of Social Psychology. Last modified November 7, 2011. www.easp.eu/activities/own/awards/tajfel.htm.

4. Tajfel, Henri, and Michael Billic. "Familiarity and Categorization in Intergroup Behavior." *Journal of Experimental Social Psychology* 10 (1974): 159–170.

5. Steinhauer, Jennifer. "Congress Nearing End of Session Where Partisan Input Impeded Output." *New York Times*, Sept. 19, 2012.

6. Bar-Tal, Daniel. "Development of Social Categories and Stereotypes in Early Childhood: The Case of 'the Arab' Concept Formation, Stereotype, and Attitudes by Jewish Children in Israel." *International Journal of Intercultural Relations* 20 (1996): 341–370.

7. Fiske, Susan T., and Shelley E. Taylor. *Social Cognition*. Boston: Addison-Wesley, 1984.

8. Tajfel, Henri, and Alan L. Wilkes. "Classification and Quantitative Judgment." *British Journal of Psychology* 54 (1963): 101–114.

9. Kelly, David J., et al. "The Other-Race Effect Develops During Infancy: Evidence of Perceptual Narrowing." *Psychological Science* 18.12 (2007): 1084–1089.

10. Pascalis, Olivier, Michelle de Haan, and Charles A. Nelson. "Is Face Processing Species-Specific During the First Year Of Life?" *Science* 296.5571 (2002): 1321–1323.

11. Ganske, Kathryn H., and Michelle R. Hebl. "Once Upon a Time There was a Math Contest: Gender Stereotyping and Memory." *Teaching of Psychology* 28 (2001): 266–268.

## Chapter 4

1. Nietzsche, Friedrich. *Human, All Too Human*. Chicago: C. H. Kerr, 1908.

2. Gray, John. *Men Are from Mars, Women Are from Venus*. New York: HarperCollins, 1993.

3. Gurian, Michael. *Boys and Girls Learn Differently!* San Francisco: Jossey-Bass, 2000.

4. Dindia, Kathryn, and Daniel J. Canary. *Sex Differences and Similarities in Communication*. New York: Taylor & Francis, 2006.

5. Schredl, Michael, and Iris Reinhard. "Gender Differences in Nightmare Frequency: A Meta-analysis." *Sleep Medicine Reviews* 15 (2011): 115–121.

6. Hyde, Janet Shibley. "The Gender Similarities Hypothesis." *American Psychologist* 60 (2005): 581.

7. Haggbloom, Steven J., et al. "The 100 Most Eminent Psychologists of the 20th Century." *Review of General Psychology* 6, no. 2 (2002): 139–152.

8. Fivush, Robyn. "Gender and Emotion in Mother-Child Conversations about the Past." *Journal of Narrative & Life History* 4 (1991): 325–341.

9. Hamilton, Mykol C., David Anderson, Michelle Broaddus, and Kate Young. "Gender Stereotyping and Under-Representation of Female Characters in 200 Popular Children's Picture Books: A Twenty-First-Century Update." *Sex Roles* 55 (2006): 757–765.

10. Eaton, Warren O., and Lesley R. Enns. "Sex Differences in Human Motor Activity Level." *Psychological Bulletin* 100 (1986): 19.

11. Furnham, Adrian, Emma Reeves, and Salima Budhani. "Parents Think Their Sons Are Brighter Than Their Daughters: Sex Differences in Parental Self-Estimations and Estimations of Their Children's Multiple Intelligences." *The Journal of Genetic Psychology* 163 (2002): 24–39.

12. Li, Qing. "Teachers' Beliefs and Gender Differences in Mathematics: A Review." *Educational Research* 41 (1999): 63–76.

13. Else-Quest, Nicole M., Janet Shibley Hyde, and Marcia C. Linn. "Cross-National Patterns of Gender Differences in Mathematics: A Meta-Analysis." *Psychological Bulletin* 136 (2010): 103.

14. Hyde, Janet S., Elizabeth Fennema, and Susan J. Lamon. "Gender Differences in Mathematics Performance: a Meta-Analysis." *Psychological Bulletin* 107 (1990): 139.

15. Hyde, Janet S., Sara M. Lindberg, Marcia C. Linn, Amy B. Ellis, and Caroline C. Williams. "Gender Similarities Characterize Math Performance." *Science* 321 (2008): 494–495.

16. Else-Quest, Nicole M., Janet Shibley Hyde, and Marcia C. Linn. "Cross-National Patterns of Gender Differences in Mathematics: A Meta-Analysis." *Psychological Bulletin* 136.1 (2010): 103–127.

17. Leaper, Campbell, and Tara E. Smith. "A Meta-Analytic Review of Gender Variations in Children's Language Use: Talkativeness, Affiliative Speech, and Assertive Speech." *Developmental Psychology* 40 (2004): 993.

18. Kling, Kristen C., Janet Shibley Hyde, Carolin J. Showers, and Brenda N. Buswell. "Gender Differences in Self-Esteem: A Meta-Analysis." *Psychological Bulletin* 125 (1999): 470–500.

19. Ricciardelli, Lina A., and Marita P. McCabe. "Children's Body Image Concerns and Eating Disturbance: A Review of the Literature." *Clinical Psychology Review* 21 (2001): 325–344.

20. Rierdan, Jill, Elissa Koff, and Margaret L. Stubbs. "A Longitudinal Analysis of Body Image as a Predictor of the Onset and Persistence of Adolescent Girls' Depression." *The Journal of Early Adolescence* 9.4 (1989): 454–466.

21. Hargreaves, Duane A., and Marika Tiggemann. "Idealized Media Images and Adolescent Body Image: 'Comparing' Boys and Girls." *Body Image* 1 (2004): 351–361.

22. Hankin, Benjamin L., Lyn Y. Abramson, Terrie E. Moffitt, Phil A. Silva, Rob McGee, and Kathryn E. Angell. "Development of Depression from Preadolescence to Young Adulthood: Emerging Gender Differences in a 10-Year Longitudinal Study." *Journal of Abnormal Psychology* 107 (1998): 128.

23. Hankin, Benjamin L., and Lyn Y. Abramson. "Development of Gender Differences in Depression: Description and Possible Explanations." *Annals of Medicine* 31 (1999): 372–379.

24. Hankin, Benjamin L., and Lyn Y. Abramson. "Development of Gender Differences in Depression: An Elaborated Cognitive Vulnerability-Transactional Stress Theory." *Psychological Bulletin* 127 (2001): 773.

25. Ibid.

26. Hyde. "Gender Similarities."

27. Cooper, Alexia, and Erica L. Smith. "Homicide Trends in the United States, 1980–2008: Annual Rates for 2009 and 2010." U. S. Department of Justice Bureau of Justice Statistics NCJ 236018 (2011).

28. Card, Noel A., et al. "Direct and Indirect Aggression During Childhood and Adolescence: A Meta-Analytic Review of Gender Differences, Intercorrelations, and Relations to Maladjustment." *Child Development* 79.5 (2008): 1185-1229.

29. Maccoby, Eleanor E. "Gender as a Social Category." *Developmental Psychology* 24 (1988): 755.

30. Hall, Judith A., and Amy G. Halberstadt. "Smiling and Gazing." *The Psychology of Gender: Advances through Meta-Analysis* (1986): 136–158.

31. Eagly, Alice H., and Maureen Crowley. "Gender and Helping Behavior: A Meta-Analytic Review of the Social Psychological Literature." *Psychological Bulletin* 100 (1986): 283–308.

32. Tzuriel, David, and Gila Egozi. "Gender Differences in Spatial Ability of Young Children: The Effects of Training and Processing Strategies." *Child Development* 81 (2010): 1417–1430.

33. Terlecki, Melissa S., and Nora S. Newcombe. "How Important Is the Digital Divide? The Relation of Computer and Videogame Usage to Gender Differences in Mental Rotation Ability." *Sex Roles* 53 (2005): 433–441.

## Chapter 5

1. http://www2.rsna.org/timssnet/media/pressreleases/pr_target.cfm?id=634. Retrieved January 21, 2014.

2. Examples of news stories: Health. http://news.health.com/2012/1⅓6/ alzheimers-may-progress-differently-in-women-men/. Retrieved January 21, 2014; Health Central. http://www.healthcentral.com/ alzheimers/c/57548/157760/Influences/. Retrieved January 21, 2014, The Morning Show: http://www.necn.com/11/28/12/Dr-Mallika-Marshall-Important-health-hea/landing_mallika.html?blockID=807039. Retrieved January 21, 2014.

3. Strand, Steve, Ian J. Deary, and Pauline Smith. "Sex Differences in Cognitive Abilities Test Scores: A UK National Picture." *British Journal of Educational Psychology* 76 (2006): 463–480.

4. Hyde, Janet Shibley. "The Gender Similarities Hypothesis." *American Psychologist* 60 (2005): 581.

5. Cohen, Jacob. *Statistical Power Analysis for the Behavioral Sciences.* San Diego, CA: Academic Press, 1969.

6. Campbell, Darren W., and Warren O. Eaton. "Sex Differences in the Activity Level of Infants." *Infant and Child Development* 8 (1999): 1–17.

7. Hyde, Janet S., and Marcia C. Linn. "Gender Differences in Verbal Ability: A Meta-Analysis." *Psychological Bulletin* 104 (1988): 53.

8. Crouter, Ann C., Susan M. McHale, and W. Todd Bartko. "Gender as an Organizing Feature in Parent-Child Relationships." *Journal of Social Issues* 49 (1993): 161–174.

## Chapter 6

1. Brizendine, Louann. *The Female Brain*. New York: Crown Publishing, 2006.
2. Young, Rebecca M., and Evan Balaban. "Psychoneuroindoctrinology." *Nature* 443 (2006): 634.
3. Lippa, Richard A. *Gender, Nature, and Nurture*. Florence: Psychology Press, 2005; Fine, Cordelia. *Delusions of Gender: How Our Minds, Society, and Neurosexism Create Difference*. New York: W.W. Norton & Co., 2011.
4. Phoenix, Charles H., Robert W. Goy, Arnold A. Gerall, and William C. Young. "Organizing Action of Prenatally Administered Testosterone Propionate on the Tissues Mediating Mating Behavior in the Female Guinea Pig." *Endocrinology* 65 (1959): 369–382.
5. Gurian, Michael. *Boys and Girls Learn Differently!* San Francisco: Jossey-Bass, 2000.
6. Sax, Leonard. *Why Gender Matters: What Parents and Teachers Need to Know about the Emerging Science of Sex Differences*. New York: Three Rivers Press, 2007; Baron-Cohen, Simon. *Essential Difference: Male and Female Brains and the Truth about Autism*. New York: Basic Books, 2004; Brizendine, Louann. *The Female Brain*. New York: Crown Publishing, 2006.
7. DeLacoste-Utamsing, Christine, and Ralph L. Holloway. "Sexual Dimorphism in the Human Corpus Callosum." *Science* 216 (1982): 1431–1432.
8. Bishop, Katherine M., and Douglas Wahlsten. "Sex Differences in the Human Corpus Callosum: Myth or Reality?" *Neuroscience & Biobehavioral Reviews* 21 (1997): 581–601; Wallentin, Mikkel. "Putative Sex Differences in Verbal Abilities and Language Cortex: A Critical Review." *Brain and Language* 108 (2009): 175–183.
9. Wallentin, Mikkel. "Putative Sex Differences in Verbal Abilities."
10. Sommer, Iris E., André Aleman, Metten Somers, Marco P. Boks, and René S. Kahn. "Sex Differences in Handedness, Asymmetry of the Planum Temporale, and Functional Language Lateralization." *Brain Research* 1206 (2008): 76–88.
11. Baron-Cohen, Simon, Michael V. Lombardo, Bonnie Auyeung, Emma Ashwin, Bhismadev Chakrabarti, and Rebecca Knickmeyer. "Why Are Autism Spectrum Conditions More Prevalent in Males?" *Plos Biology* 9 (2011): 1–10.
12. Connellan, Jennifer, Simon Baron-Cohen, Sally Wheelwright, Anna Batki, and Jag Ahluwalia. "Sex Differences in Human Neonatal Social Perception." *Infant Behavior and Development* 23 (2000): 113–118.
13. Moir, Anne, and David Jessel. *Brain Sex*. New York: Dell Publishing, 1992.
14. Gurian. *Boys and Girls Learn Differently!*
15. http://itre.cis.upenn.edu/~myl/languagelog/archives/003923.html.
16. Edwards, David A. "Early Androgen Stimulation and Aggressive Behavior in Male and Female Mice." *Physiology & Behavior* 4.3 (1969): 333–338.
17. Bennett, Craig M., M. B. Miller, and G. L. Wolford. "Neural Correlates of Interspecies Perspective Taking in the Post-Mortem Atlantic Salmon: An Argument for Multiple Comparisons Correction." *NeuroImage* 47 (2009): S125.
18. Eliot, Lise. *Pink Brain, Blue Brain*. Boston: Houghton Mifflin Harcourt, 2009.

19. Jordan-Young, Rebecca M. *Brain Storm: The Flaws in the Science of Sex Differences.* Cambridge: Harvard University Press, 2010.

20. Servin, Anna, Anna Nordenstrom, Agne Larsson, and Gunilla Bohlin. "Prenatal Androgens and Gender-Typed Behavior: A Study of Girls with Mild and Severe Forms of Congenital Adrenal Hyperplasia." *Developmental Psychology* 39 (2003): 440–449.

21. Ibid.

22. De Vries, Geert J. "Sex Differences in Adult and Developing Brains." *Endocrinology* 145 (2004): 1063–1068.

23. Hines, Melissa. "Gender Development and the Human Brain." *Annual Review of Neuroscience* 34 (2011): 69–88.

24. Birch, Eileen, and David Stager. "The Critical Period for Surgical Treatment of Dense Congenital Unilateral Cataract." *Investigative Ophthalmology and Visual Science* 37 (1996): 1532–1538.

25. Kersh, Joanne, Beth M. Casey, and Jessica Mercer Young. "Research on Spatial Skills and Block Building in Girls and Boys." *Contemporary Perspectives on Mathematics in Early Childhood Education* (2008): 233–251.

26. Andersen, Susan L. "Trajectories of Brain Development: Point of Vulnerability or Window of Opportunity?" *Neuroscience & Biobehavioral Reviews* 27.1 (2003): 3–18.

27. Fox, Nathan A., Amie A. Hane, and Daniel S. Pine. "Plasticity for Affective Neurocircuitry: How the Environment Affects Gene Expression." *Current Directions in Psychological Science* 16.1 (2007): 1–5.

## Chapter 7

1. Seuss. *The Sneetches and Other Stories.* London: HarperCollins UK, 2006, 3.

2. Ibid, 5.

3. Serbin, Lisa A., and Jane M. Connor. "Sex-Typing of Children's Play Preferences and Patterns of Cognitive Performance." *The Journal of Genetic Psychology* 134 (1979): 315–316.

4. Bauer, Patricia J., and Molly J. Coyne. "When the Name Says It All: Preschoolers' Recognition and Use of the Gendered Nature of Common Proper Names." *Social Development* 6 (1997): 271–291.

5. Bradbard, Marilyn R., and Richard C. Endsley. "The Effects of Sex-Typed Labeling on Preschool Children's Information-Seeking and Retention." *Sex Roles* 9 (1983): 247–260.

6. Montemayor, Raymond. "Children's Performance in a Game and Their Attraction to It as a Function of Sex-Typed Labels." *Child Development* (1974): 152–156.

7. Maccoby, Eleanor E. "Gender as a Social Category." *Developmental Psychology* 24 (1988): 755.

8. Fagot, Beverly I., Mary D. Leinbach, and Richard Hagan. "Gender Labeling and the Adoption of Sex-Typed Behaviors." *Developmental Psychology* 22 (1986): 440–443.

9. Robnett, Rachael D., and Joshua E. Susskind. "Who Cares about Being Gentle? The Impact of Social Identity and the Gender of One's Friends on Children's Display of Same-Gender Favoritism." *Sex Roles* 63 (2010): 820–832.

10. Aronson, Elliot. *The Social Animal*. New York: Macmillan, 2003.
11. Banerjee, Robin, and Vicki Lintern. "Boys Will Be Boys: The Effect of Social Evaluation Concerns on Gender-Typing." *Social Development* 9 (2000): 397–408.
12. Lipson, Jodi. "Hostile Hallways: Bullying, Teasing, and Sexual Harassment in School." AAUW Educational Foundation, 1111 Sixteenth Street, NW, Washington, DC 20036, 2001.
13. Leaper, Campbell, and Christia Spears Brown. "Perceived Experiences with Sexism Among Adolescent Girls." *Child Development* 79 (2008): 685–704.
14. Chiodo, Debbie, David A. Wolfe, Claire Crooks, Ray Hughes, and Peter Jaffe. "Impact of Sexual Harassment Victimization by Peers on Subsequent Adolescent Victimization and Adjustment: A Longitudinal Study." *Journal Of Adolescent Health* 45 (2009): 246–252.
15. Martin, Carol Lynn. "The Role of Cognition in Understanding Gender Effects." *Advances in Child Development and Behavior* 23 (1991): 113–164.
16. Signorella, Margaret L., Rebecca S. Bigler, and Lynn S. Liben. "A Meta-Analysis of Children's Memories for Own-Sex and Other-Sex Information." *Journal of Applied Developmental Psychology* 18 (1997): 429–445.
17. Liben, Lynn S., and Margaret L. Signorella. "Gender-Schematic Processing in Children: The Role of Initial Interpretations of Stimuli." *Developmental Psychology* 29 (1993): 141.
18. Weisgram, Erica S., and Rebecca S. Bigler. "Girls and Science Careers: The Role of Altruistic Values and Attitudes about Scientific Tasks." *Journal of Applied Developmental Psychology* 27 (2006): 326–348.
19. Bigler, Rebecca S., Andrea E. Arthur, Julie Milligan Hughes, and Meagan M. Patterson. "The Politics of Race and Gender: Children's Perceptions of Discrimination and the US Presidency." *Analyses of Social Issues and Public Policy* 8 (2008): 83–112.
20. Ryan, Allison M., Margaret H. Gheen, and Carol Midgley. "Why Do Some Students Avoid Asking for Help? An Examination of the Interplay Among Students' Academic Efficacy, Teachers' Social-Emotional Role, and the Classroom Goal Structure." *Journal of Educational Psychology* 90 (1998): 528–535.

## Chapter 8

1. Lytton, Hugh, and David M. Romney. "Parents' Differential Socialization of Boys and Girls: A Meta-Analysis." *Psychological Bulletin* 109, no. 2 (1991): 267–296.
2. Nash, A., and R. Krawczyk. "Boys' and Girls' Rooms Revisited: The Contents of Boys' and Girls' Rooms in the 1990s." Talk at Conference on Human Development, Pittsburgh, Pennsylvania, 1994.
3. Culp, Rex E., Alicia S. Cook, and Patricia C. Housley. "A Comparison of Observed and Reported Adult-Infant Interactions: Effects of Perceived Sex." *Sex Roles* 9.4 (1983): 475–479.
4. Fivush, Robyn, Melissa A. Brotman, Janine P. Buckner, and Sherryl H. Goodman. "Gender Differences in Parent-Child Emotion Narratives." *Sex Roles* 42, no. 3–4 (2000): 233–253.

5. Perry, David C., Jean C. Williard, and Louise C. Perry. "Peers' Perceptions of the Consequences That Victimized Children Provide Aggressors." *Child Development* 61 (1990): 1310–1325.

6. Eccles, Jacquelynne S., Carol Freedman-Doan, Pam Frome, Janis Jacobs, and Kwang Suk Yoon. "Gender-Role Socialization in the Family: A Longitudinal Approach." *The Developmental Social Psychology of Gender*, 336–360. Mahwah, NJ: Lawrence Erlbaum Associates Publishers, 2000.

7. Ibid.

8. Tenenbaum, Harriet R., and Campbell Leaper. "Parent-Child Conversations about Science: The Socialization of Gender Inequities?" *Developmental Psychology* 39 (2003): 34–46.

9. Bhanot, Ruchi, and Jasna Jovanovic. "Do Parents' Academic Gender Stereotypes Influence Whether They Intrude on Their Children's Homework?" *Sex Roles* 52 (2005), no. 9–10: 597–607.

10. Chang, Alicia, Catherine M. Sandhofer, and Christia S. Brown. "Gender Biases in Early Number Exposure to Preschool-Aged Children." *Journal of Language and Social Psychology* 30, no. 4 (2011): 440–450.

11. Langlois, Judith H., and A. Chris Downs. "Mothers, Fathers, and Peers as Socialization Agents of Sex-Typed Play Behaviors in Young Children." *Child Development* (1980): 1237–1247.

12. Harnick, Sheldon, and Mary Rodgers. "William's Doll." Performed by Alan Alda and Marlo Thomas (based on the children's book of the same name). *Free to Be ... You and Me* CD (1972). Arista Records.

13. Caldera, Yvonne M., Aletha C. Huston, and Marion O'Brien. "Social Interactions and Play Patterns of Parents and Toddlers with Feminine, Masculine, and Neutral Toys." *Child Development* (1989): 70–76.

## Chapter 9

1. Rosenthal, Robert. "On the Social Psychology of the Psychological Experiment: The Experimenter's Hypothesis as Unintended Determinant of Experimental Results." *American Psychologist* 1s: 268–283.

2. Rosenthal, Robert, and Lenore Jacobson. *Pygmalion in the Classroom: Teacher Expectation and Pupils' Intellectual Development*. Austin, TX: Rinehart and Winston, 1968.

3. Castelli, Luigi, Cristina De Dea, and Drew Nesdale. "Learning Social Attitudes: Children's Sensitivity to the Nonverbal Behaviors of Adult Models During Interracial Interactions." *Personality and Social Psychology Bulletin* 34 (2008): 1504–1513.

4. Hothersall, David. *History of Psychology*. New York: McGraw-Hill, 2004.

5. Eccles, Jacquelynne S., Allan Wigfield, Constance A. Flanagan, Christy Miller, David A. Reuman, and Doris Yee. "Self-Concepts, Domain Values, and Self-Esteem: Relations and Changes at Early Adolescence." *Journal of Personality* 57 (1989): 283–310.

6. Caldera, Yvonne M. "Paternal Involvement and Infant-Father Attachment: A Q-Set Study." *Fathering* 2 (2004): 191–210.

7. Hankin, Benjamin L., and Lyn Y. Abramson. "Development of Gender Differences in Depression: Description and Possible Explanations." *Annals of medicine* 31.6 (1999): 372–379.
8. Clark, Levina, and Marika Tiggemann. "Sociocultural and Individual Psychological Predictors of Body Image in Young Girls: A Prospective Study." *Developmental Psychology* 44 (2008): 1124–1134.
9. Smolak, Linda, and Michael P. Levine. "Body Image in Children." *Body Image, Eating Disorders, and Obesity in Youth: Assessment, Prevention, and Treatment* (2001): 41–66.
10. Dittmar, Helga, Emma Halliwell, and Suzanne Ive. "Does Barbie Make Girls Want to Be Thin? The Effect of Experimental Exposure to Images of Dolls on the Body Image of 5-to 8-Year-Old Girls." *Developmental Psychology* 42.2 (2006): 283.
11. Bell, Lee Anne. "Something's Wrong Here and It's Not Me: Challenging the Dilemmas That Block Girls' Success." *Journal for the Education of the Gifted* 12 (1989): 118–30.
12. Ridolfo, Heather, Valerie Chepp, and Melissa A. Milkie. "Race and Girls' Self-Evaluations: How Mothering Matters." *Sex Roles* (2013): 1–14.

## Chapter 10

1. Danaher, Kelly, and Christian S. Crandall. "Stereotype Threat in Applied Settings Re-Examined." *Journal of Applied Social Psychology* 38 (2008): 1639–1655.
2. Steele, Claude M., and Joshua Aronson. "Stereotype Threat and the Intellectual Test Performance of African Americans." *Journal of Personality and Social Psychology* 69 (1995): 797–811.
3. Steele, Claude M. *Whistling Vivaldi: How Stereotypes Affect Us.* New York: W.W. Norton and Co., 2011.
4. Hartley, Bonny L., and Robbie M. Sutton. "A Stereotype Threat Account of Boys' Academic Underachievement." *Child Development* (2013).
5. Davies, Paul G., Steven J. Spencer, Diane M. Quinn, and Rebecca Gerhardstein. "Consuming Images: How Television Commercials That Elicit Stereotype Threat Can Restrain Women Academically and Professionally." *Personality and Social Psychology Bulletin* 28 (2002): 1615–1628.
6. Davies, Paul G., Steven J. Spencer, and Claude M. Steele. "Clearing the Air: Identity Safety Moderates the Effects of Stereotype Threat on Women's Leadership Aspirations." *Journal of Personality and Social Psychology* 88 (2005): 276–287.
7. Cohen, Geoffrey L., Julio Garcia, Nancy Apfel, and Allison Master. "Reducing the Racial Achievement Gap: A Social-Psychological Intervention." *Science* 313 (2006): 1307–1310.

## Chapter 11

1. Quotations from David B. Tyack and Elisabeth Hansot. *Learning Together: A History of Coeducation in American Public Schools.* New York: Russell Sage Foundation, 1992, 159, 180.

2. Nolan, Kay. "School to Explore Science of Gender; Arrowhead Will Offer Separate Classes for Boys, Girls." *Milwaukee Sentinel Journal*, March 9, 2006, 3B.

3. American Civil Liberties Union. 3:08-cv-00004-CRS; Breckinridge County Public School District. Civil Action No. 3:08-cv-00004-CRS.

4. National Association for Single Sex Public Education Sixth International Conference, Las Vegas, Nevada, October 9–10, 2010.

5. National Center for Education Statistics. "U.S. Performance Across International Assessments of Student Achievement." http://nces.ed.gov/programs/coe/analysis/2009-index.asp.

6. Sax, Leonard. *Why Gender Matters: What Parents and Teachers Need to Know about the Emerging Science of Sex Differences.* Random House Digital, Inc., 2007.

7. Maccoby, Eleanor E., and Carol Nagy Jacklin. *The Psychology of Sex Differences.* Palo Alto, CA: Stanford University Press, 1974.

8. Dennis McFadden quoted by Eliot, Lise. *Pink Brain, Blue Brain.* Boston: Houghton Mifflin Harcourt 2009, 326.

9. Mark Liberman quoted by Eliot, Lise. *Pink Brain, Blue Brain.* Boston: Houghton Mifflin Harcourt 2009, 327.

10. American Civil Liberties Union. 3:08-cv-00004-CRS.

11. Leaper, Campbell, and Christia Spears Brown. "Perceived Experiences with Sexism Among Adolescent Girls." *Child Development* 79 (2008): 685–704.

12. Bigler, Rebecca. "Reducing Sexism in Schools: Is Single-Sex Schooling a Solution?" Paper presented at the Annual Conference for American Education Research Association, Vancouver, Canada, 2012.

13. Hayes, Amy Roberson, Erin E. Pahlke, and Rebecca S. Bigler. "The Efficacy of Single-Sex Education: Testing for Selection and Peer Quality Effects." *Sex Roles* 65 (2011): 693–703.

14. Singh, Kusum, Claire Vaught, and Ethel W. Mitchell. "Single-Sex Classes and Academic Achievement in Two Inner-City Schools." *Journal of Negro Education* (1998): 157–167.

15. Mael, Fred, Alex Alonso, Doug Gibson, Kelly Rogers, and Mark Smith. "Single-Sex Versus Coeducational Schooling: A Systematic Review. Doc# 2005-01." Washington, DC: U.S. Department of Education, 2005.

16. Salomone, Rosemary C. *Same, Different, Equal: Rethinking Single-Sex Schooling.* New Haven, CT: Yale University Press, 2003.

17. Thompson, Terri, and Charles S. Ungerleider. "Single Sex Schooling: Final Report." Ottawa: Canadian Centre for Knowledge Mobilisation, 2004.

18. Bigler. "Reducing Sexism in Schools."

19. Kornell, Nate. "Optimizing Learning Using Flashcards: Spacing Is More Effective Than Cramming." *Applied Cognitive Psychology* 23 (2009): 1297–1317.

20. Datnow, Amanda, Lea Hubbard, and Elisabeth Woody. *Is Single Gender Schooling Viable in the Public Sector?: Lessons from California's Pilot Program.* Toronto: OISE, 2001.

21. Halpern, Diane. Report of Diane Halpern. *Issues of Single-Sex Education.* Available at www.aclu.org/files/assets/Expert_Report_-_Diane_Halpern.pdf.

# About the Author

Shaun Ring, 2013

Dr. Christia Spears Brown is an Associate Professor of Developmental Psychology at the University of Kentucky and has spent the past two decades examining how gender affects the lives of children. She has published widely in top scientific journals on issues related to gender development and academics.

Her work on gender issues has been featured on National Public Radio, *CBS Evening News with Katie Couric*, *Ms. Magazine*, *Slate*, and numerous magazines and newspapers. She is a member of the Society for Research in Child Development, the American Council for Co-Educational Schools, and frequently speaks at national conferences regarding gender issues and child development. She earned her Ph.D. in 2003 at The University of Texas at Austin. She also has two daughters, Maya and Grace; a husband, Kris; and a dog, Coco.

# Index

# More Parenting Titles from Ten Speed Press

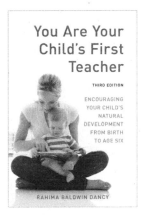

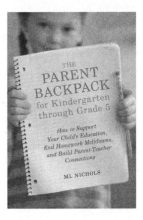

**You Are Your Child's First Teacher,
Third Edition**
Encouraging Your Child's Natural
Development from Birth to Age Six
Rahima Baldwin Dancy
$12.99 (Canada $13.99)
ISBN: 978-1-60774-302-6
eBook ISBN: 978-1-60774-303-3

**The Parent Backpack for
Kindergarten through Grade 5**
How to Support Your Child's Education,
End Homework Meltdowns, and Build
Parent-Teacher Connections
ML Nichols
$15.99 (Canada: $16.99)
ISBN: 978-1-60774-474-0
eBook ISBN: 978-1-60774-475-7

**Raising a Self-Reliant Child**
A Back-to-Basics Parenting Plan
from Birth to Age 6
Dr. Alanna Levine
$15.99 (Canada $18.99)
ISBN: 978-1-60774-350-7
eBook ISBN: 978-1-60774-351-4

AVAILABLE
EVERYWHERE
BOOKS ARE SOLD

TEN SPEED PRESS
www.tenspeed.com